East to Eden?

East to Eden?

Religion and the Dynamics of Social Change

CHARLES CORWIN

WILLIAM B. EERDMANS PUBLISHING COMPANY
Grand Rapids, Michigan

Library of Congress Catalog Card Number: 77-184693
ISBN 0-8028-1444-1
Printed in the United States of America

TO

CATHY AND JIM

Preface

The Japanese train halted amid a flurry of sparks from braked wheels. Passersby on the platform came running and peered over the edge, searching for something—or someone. I turned to a bystander, asking, "What happened?" "Oh, a drunk fell over the platform and was trapped under the wheels. Why they let those *otora* through the gates I'll never know." *Otora* literally means "great tiger," but in Japanese parlance means "wild drunkard." The drunkard in this case was extricated from beneath the train, shaken but unhurt. Enroute home I mulled over the bystander's words, "Why they let these tigers through. . . ." I recalled pictures of American highway patrolmen making tipplers walk the center line of the pavement. Why not paint a white line in front of every ticket gate and have ticket-punchers ask flushed commuters to walk the line? Could not accidents be cut down and the Japanese railway system end its traditional service as public tiger refuge?

The next day I visited the Takada-no-baba stationmaster and related the incident. A similar accident had occurred in his station the night before, killing a young man returning from his first drinking bout. The distraught stationmaster listened intently to my suggestion, picked up the phone, and told the National Railway authorities about the white line and its possibilities. I returned to his station in a few days, and he startled me with these words: "We have never used a white line painted on the station floor to eliminate the worst drunks. We want to give it a try, but er . . . uh . . . we wish to ask a favor of you. Would you and your students implement this?" I was thunderstruck! Ridiculous! An American standing with Japanese students in a busy train station at night, stopping drunks, getting them somehow to walk a white line. But I bargained. "All right. If we keep the tigers out, will you then take proper steps throughout the metropolitan system to cut down public drunkenness?" "Yes," was the reply.

We went to work over the New Year's holiday. The experiment became a spectacle of the absurd. Some drunks, convulsed with laughter, tiptoed down the elusive white line like playful kittens. Others roared at the interruption or lunged menacingly at us. But the results were promising. Getting wind of the trap, drunks began avoiding Takada-no-baba, and no accidents were reported during the ten days. News media and television began telling about the work of these students. My wife and I put on a skit before fifty Tokyo stationmasters to demonstrate the plight commuters are in when menaced by these drunks. Shortly thereafter the Japanese government moved into action, inaugurating a new police force to patrol trains at night. Japanese commuters would be protected from the uncivility and abuse of *otora.*

The outcome pleased me but raised certain questions. Why was I a foreigner asked to help? How does social reform begin? With whom? Why had this obvious problem gone unnoticed by sensitive Japanese? Have not their religions spoken out against it? Leaving these questions unanswered, I took another look at Eastern societies. How have they changed during the modern era? What ideas have produced social reform? Hinduism and Islam in India; Confucianism, Buddhism, and Taoism in China; Shinto, Buddhism and Confucianism in Japan—certainly these dominant religions and philosophies have brought tremendous changes to these countries. They have served as matrixes for culture, handmaidens of states, spiritual cohesives for community life. Or have they? Christianity, however, has been persistently resisted by these cultures, disdained as an interloper, winning few converts. Social efforts by national churches have been miniscule and innocuous. Or have they?

When I came from Japan to Santa Barbara in 1969 I discovered that American college students, now being taught Eastern ways of liberation from social repression, are asking similar questions. What is the Eastern way of life? Will it work in the West? Will Eastern philosophy take us back to nature, deliver us from a mentality that can tolerate violence but not eros, turn us from materialism? Have those ideas worked in Asia? Which ideas actually brought about radical social changes in Asia, Eastern ideas or Western?

This book grew out of a seminar on Asian problems I held at Westmont College in the spring of 1970. I want to thank Westmont for the research grant given me to continue this study and make the findings of our seminar available to others. I am also deeply grateful to Dr. Immanuel Hsü, Professor of History, Dr. Herbert Fingarette, Professor of Philosophy, Dr. M. V. Lamberti, Associate Professor of History, Dr. S. N. Ray, Professor of History, all from the University of California at Santa Barbara, for their academic counsel in the preparation and correction of the manuscript. The errors and omissions are my own responsibility.

C.C.

Contents

Preface 7

Introduction 13

1. India 21

2. China 51

3. Japan 95

4. Dynamics for Change 153

Index 183

Introduction

John Ciardi, in the *Saturday Review* of October 24, 1970, tells of an amusing encounter he had with one of America's flower children:

> He said he had liked my poems before all poetry began to give him bad vibrations, and he had dropped in because he happened to be passing by. He was like on the road and he was trying to find himself. In paraphrase, as I soon gathered, that meant his psyche had no time left over for holding down a job. It had its consciousness to expand and its thing to find. Finding its thing was directly related to finding something called "Allness." Not only was it necessary to find both its thing and Allness's thing, but then Allness and its thing had to be related to the psyche's thing.
>
> "On equal terms?" I asked. "Like flower to sun, man. The sun's bigger and older and way out there and goes on like to infinity. And the flower is only like now, this instant, but in the infinity of the instant they are like equal, like one *from* the other and *to* the other and *in* the other. Like essence, man. And when this instant is over, right behind it comes another instant as infinite as every other instant. And even if everything now was closed, I mean like without being an infinite, it would still take all of infinity to think about it, I mean to really get with it."

If these thoughts are fairly representative, then obviously the ideology for America's new counter-culture is Eastern, not Western. But why are young people abandoning Western thought and institutions for these esoteric Eastern ideas? Their reasoning goes something like this: The industrial, materialistic, technological society of the West is a machine that crushes hopes for self-realization. Undeniably, this machine produces many "conveniences." But since Western society measures success by one's accumulation of these conveniences, man must lose himself in the operation of the machine. Eastern religion offers self-realization through contentment and contemplation. It deserves a try. Western philosophy has heightened not relieved the tensions of modern life. Existentialism, for example, despite its plea for man to create life-meaning in the face of a purposeless cosmos by decisive acts, has engendered a sense of futility, meaninglessness, and alienation. American Christianity survives only by abandoning its critical, supra-cultural position to an abhorrent system of society; it has muffled its prophetic voice by becoming a spokesman for the establishment. Young people today are disenchanted with Christianity's complacency, irrelevance, and pat answers to the momentous questions of life. Eastern religions offer liberation from a moralistic Ego that must perform properly to perpetuate society. They merge man into his environment by affirming a natural-spiritual ecology of rhythm, while eschewing violence and materialism.

The American journey to the East is actually a search for the occult, the magical, the bizarre, the exotic—anything that will assuage thirst for transcendency or give religious dimension and idealization for a random, antinomian, beyond-morality life style. Zen, for example, begins at the point where there is nothing more to seek, grasp for, or attain. It is the cult of the absurd, the ritual of nose tweeks and leg pulls, the philosophy of non-mind, no-thought, no-striving. The paradoxes and witticisms of Zen have become as familiar to youth as the Christian catechism.[1] In short, it has become religious psychotherapy for a generation boxed-in by technocracy. Suffocating and restless in Western thought structures, youth are fleeing to the philosophy of "no answer." "Zen is to religion what a flat garden is to a garden. It knows no god, no afterlife, no good and no evil, as the flat garden knows no flowers, herbs or shrubs. . . . When a disciple asks, 'What is Zen?', the master's traditional answer is 'Three pounds of flax,' or 'A decaying noodle,' or 'A toilet stick,' or a whack on the pupil's head."[2] Indian mysticism also has its appeal—not Vedantic absorption into the wholly other but a this-worldly mysticism that transports body and mind into phantasy, eroticism, or self-affirmation. In this way Eastern religions are providing the theology for America's revolutionary "counter-culture," as Roszak asserts: "The dissenting young have indeed got religion. Not the brand of religion Billy Graham or William Buckley would like to see the young crusading for—but religion nonetheless. What began with Zen has now rapidly, perhaps too rapidly, proliferated into a phantasmagoria of exotic religiosity."[3]

Can religiosity counter anything? Religion and social change seem poles apart. The one speaks of contemplation, flight to another world; the other, of action, confrontation in this world. But what is religion? Before youth adopt Eastern religion as theology for their counter-culture, they must proceed beyond symbol to reality. To safeguard us from the naive assumption that the essences of Eastern religions can be found in neat English translations, we will approach religion from the human side. When a man is grasped by an *ultimate concern,* his orientation to that concern can be characterized as religious experience. Ul-

[1] Theodore Roszak, *The Making of a Counter Culture,* Doubleday and Company, New York, 1969, p. 131.

[2] Arthur Koestler, *The Lotus and the Robot,* The Macmillan Company, New York, 1961, pp. 232-233.

[3] Roszak, pp. 138-139.

timate concern, said Paul Tillich, is unconditional, absolute, and unqualified; it is what gives meaning, purpose and direction to life. Lesser concerns are focused on a goal by this dominating, pervasive interest. The ultimate concern concept (instead of "religious object" or "god") says that the meaning of religion is not discovered in man's language but in his response. It further says that there are many concerns in every culture, but that the greatest one is religious in character. For the greatest concern evokes faith from those who accept its claim. This faith expects self-fulfillment once surrender is made to that concern. Thus, since ultimate concern directs lesser concerns and radical social change is one of these lesser concerns, it follows that religion and social change are intimately related. History supports this thesis: religion has powerfully affected Asian social reform movements in at least four ways. Negatively, religion has (1) spawned cultural values that repress man's creative self, causing him to clamor for social reform (India), or (2) been used by reigning elites to abort social reform (nineteenth-century China). Positively, religion has (3) diverted revolutionary energy into constructive social reform (Meiji Japan) or (4) provided the symbols and motivations for precipitating social change.

The question, then, is not *if* religion has affected social change but *how?* Some religious ideas have fostered change, others have hindered it. To determine which ideas have fostered social change we must probe deeper into Eastern religious philosophies. But stepping into Oriental thought, we trip on the doorstep of an elementary question, namely, "What is man?" Soaring to the impersonal mind of the universe—the Indian Oversoul (*Brahman*)—or grasping the rational principle of the cosmos—the Chinese *li*—or being caught up in the effortless way of the *Tao,* or going the other way into the heart of nature via the Japanese *kami,* or tearing off layers of illusion to discover the non-self (*muga*) of Zen, students of Eastern thought are taught the causes of suffering and social malaise, ways of deliverance and happiness. But they quickly lose their way in the corridors of Eastern anthropologies. The hallways are many and lead to no central room of agreement. How often have Chinese scholars, in reflecting over the causes of dynastic decline, attributed such decline to a false interpretation of man on the part of Chinese lawmakers. For example, Han scholars like Chia I (201-169 B.C.) inveighed against the Legalists of the Chin dynasty (221-206 B.C.) for their overly pessimistic views of man's nature. Such pessimism, they pointed out, led to a proliferation of harsh laws and cruel punishments that made life for the common man intolerable. The Japanese concept of man extrapolated from Shinto-Confucian-Buddhist ideas is an enigma. Within the social nexus of family, firm, community, or nation the Japanese man finds himself. But once outside this circle he is seized with doubts. Ambivalence shadows him. To some he is flamboyant, lavish, domineering; to others, retiring, penurious, docile. Man in India finds himself imprisoned within a stratified society, unable to escape from class distinctions determined before birth. Only the Law (*dharma*) teaches him how to ignore his chains and flee to the perfect freedom of Brahman.

But have Western inquiries into the nature of man reached any consensus? Western thinkers agree on but one point: however one may attempt to capture the biped called man within specialized fences—whether in psychology, economics, biology or sociology—he eludes his pursuers. Their many definitions of man—for example, "the witness to the mystery of being" (Peters), "the nature that is able to will" (Schiller), "the depraved animal" (Klage), "the animated being which experiences" (Waitz), "the creature who bores himself" (Sombart), "the only animal for whom his own existence is a problem" (Fromm), "the being who is the object of his own reflection" (Chardin)—all these conjure up the scene of blind men groping about an elephant, giving various and ingenious explanations none of which fully explain the creature. Deterministic explanations of man such as "the social animal," "a psyche driven by sexual appetites," or "a member of a class whose goals and mores determine his values" fix boundaries only to have them trespassed by the logotherapists with their new dimension—the will to meaning. Man is still the "unknown," says Alexis Carrel, echoing the ancient verdict of Democritus: "Man is something we all know. But if we consider our own self, then we must say, 'What man is, no one knows'."[4] Max Scheler says, "All the problems of philosophy go back to the basic question, 'What is man?' "[5]

If this is true for philosophy, how much more for sociology? Ideas for dynamic living and social reform, then, should be found in the milieu of correct answers to that central question, "What is man?" Such answers should satisfy man's aspirations as a finite creature whose thought processes transcend his finitude. This noetic power enables man to reflect upon himself, evaluate the existential moment, leave the mundane and project himself into frontiers of new experience. Thus, before turning to Eastern religion or Western existentialism for self-fulfillment, we should heed what these systems say about man and his role in society. To change society you must change man, and to change man you must understand him.

The following pages will make a phenomenological study of man as he appears in the Indian, Chinese and Japanese traditions. Phenomenology is the examination and classification of what appears. What appears in our

[4] Quoted by G. C. Berkouwer in *Man, The Image of God,* Wm. B. Eerdmans Publishing Company, Grand Rapids, 1962, p. 19.

[5] *Ibid.,* p. 12.

case is man. He walks out of the writings of religious men whose ideas about man were corollaries to their concepts of ultimate reality. The relation of these religious ultimacies to their societies can be subsumed under the word "dominance." In India it is the dominance of pure essence; in China, the dominance of an heavenly hierarchal order; in Japan, the dominance of a man-in-the cosmos ethos. To test the validity of these dominances three questions will be put to their religious sources: (1) What is man? (2) What is his role in society? (3) What is his life goal? Answers to these crucial questions should unveil the nature of those dominances. Further, these answers will arrange themselves into a recognizable mosaic for living. Is it for this we are searching? Will these dominances provide a potential for social transformation? This brings up another question: "Have these ideas about man been productive of social reform?" To answer this we will pause at historical turning points in each culture. We will examine critical episodes wherein social reform was *the* issue. Who were the leaders of social reform in Asia? How was their thinking crystallized? What new ideas spurred them into action? Or what ideas pulled up the reins on reform? What were the religious overtones of those ideas?

In the last chapter we leave phenomenology and make value judgments by taking a closer look at the relation between Eastern religious ultimacies and their societies. If the answers concerning man given by these ultimacies elevate him, increase his capacity, give him the impetus, purpose, and ethic for a radically dynamic life, then we will have to accept these ultimacies as worthy of self-commitment. For by making such a commitment I insure my chances for self-fulfillment. A rational man will not commit himself to a religious idea that integrates him into culture but fails at self-fulfillment. Finally one more option as a dynamic for social reform will be discussed—Christian radicalism. This should prepare us for the final question: Are the dynamics for social reform to be found in Eastern religion or in Christian radicalism?

1

India

Hinduism is both a way of life and a highly organized socio-religious system. It is free from any dogmatic affirmations about the nature of divinity, for the core of Indian religion is never felt to depend on the existence or nonexistence of God, or on whether there is one God or many. One may be a good Hindu and embrace monism, monotheism, polytheism, or even atheism. The Hindus themselves call their religion the *sanatana dharma* or "eternal law." The word *dharma* is used in two general senses in the great Hindu texts: "law" and "religion." Although Hindus take pride in the fact that their religion is free from dogmatic assumptions, there are certain presuppositions in post-Vedic Hinduism which are rarely, if ever, disputed. One is the doctrine of transmigration or rebirth of souls. All sects and all philosophical schools accept this idea. This doctrine presupposes another generally accepted hypothesis about cause and effect, for it says that the condition into which the individual soul is reborn is itself the result of good or bad actions performed in former lives. This is the law of *karma* or "action," which states that any action whatsoever is the effect of a cause and in turn becomes the cause of a further effect, much like billiard balls set in motion by one another. The whole process goes by the name of *samsara,* the course or revolution to which all phenomenal existence adheres. And *samsara* itself is subject to and conditioned by endless cause, the *dharma* of the universe. With this *dharma* there is neither beginning nor end, either for the sum total of existence, the macrocosm, or the individual soul, the microcosm. Everything is shackled to *samsara* by the fetters of time and the fetters of human desire, the desire above all to live and to act. Time itself is a revolving wheel returning ever again to the point of zero time. Thus there can be neither purpose nor salvation in history. These presuppositions are accepted as sober fact by most Hindu sects and philosophical schools. But all schools find these assumptions profoundly unsatisfactory and disquieting.

This being the case, it is the aim of every Hindu to escape from the wheel of time and the wheel of action. That such an escape is possible is affirmed by all schools. It is called *moksha* or *mukti,* terms best translated as "release," "escape," "liberation," or "emancipation." However, the *manner* by which this blessed state can be achieved and the *nature* of the soul that has fought itself free from the fetters of time and desire are matters about which Hindus sharply differ.

Historically, Hinduism may be divided into four distinct periods. The earliest is called the Vedic period (c. 1200-900 B.C.), the literary monument of which is the *Rig-Veda,* a collection of ritualistic hymns to cultural heroes who became personifications of nature, such as Indra the storm god or Agni the fire god. The primitive foundations of this Vedic period were in part Indo-European. Aryan tribes marauding India during the second millennium before Christ brought with them well-organized religious beliefs which survived and later, with some modification, surfaced in classical Hinduism. Also Hinduism assimilated some pre-Aryan institutions indigenous to India. This pre-Aryan and pre-historical civilization was discovered at Mohenjodaro in the Indus basin of northwest India and is called the Harappa culture (third-second millennium B.C.). A few characteristics of this proto-Hindu culture were the worship of a mother goddess, the veneration of a horned god in the posture of a yogi, the keeping of ritual emblems of certain vegetables or animals, and the worship of phallic symbols. Though the Aryans and Harappa people were implacable enemies at the onset of these invasions, within several centuries both cultures were amalgamated into the distinct culture of the Vedic period, a culture marked by nature worship, fertility cults, ritual, and sacrifice to functional gods.

The second period of Hinduism was characterized by transcendentalism and found its expression in the Upanishadic literature (c. 900-500 B.C.). Primitive nature worship gave way to pantheistic monism. The "many" are drawn up into the "one" or wholly identified with the One called Brahman. Brahman, which was originally the magic of the sacred word in the Vedic hymns, became ultimate reality. Brahman has been variously translated "the great It," "the impersonal Mind of the universe," "the Oversoul," "the Allness," "the Suchness of the universe." This Allness cannot be described in human terms; anthropological descriptions of Brahman distort and limit the nature of the great Neuter. During the Upanishadic period a great philosophical leap was made: the individual soul of man (*atman*) was identified with Brahman according to the formula, "That art thou." This meant in effect that the gods of the Vedic period were dethroned and the human soul set up in their place. Man's true self became divine.

I should add in passing that there has been a revival of interest in the teachings of this second period of Hinduism both in India and the Western world. For this aspect of

Hinduism emphasizes *moksha,* the liberation of the human soul from time, space, and matter. Humanistic psychology in the West attempts to free man from the repression of social conditioning. Allan Watts in his *Psychotherapy East and West* says, "When a man no longer confuses himself with the definition of himself that others have given him, he is at once universal and unique. He is universal by virtue of the inseparability of his organism from the cosmos."[1] As the self is liberated from social conditioning and allowed to run free in the cosmos, "ethics are transformed from the rules of repression into the technique of expression and morality becomes the aesthetics of behavior."[2] Such ideas find their matrix in this second period of Hinduism. "Finding one's thing" or "expanding one's consciousness by being related to the Allness" are simply modern jargon for ancient Upanishadic thought.

The third, and perhaps the most important, phase in Hinduism was characterized by the development of strong monotheistic trends on the one hand and the crystallization of the caste system on the other (c. 500 B.C.-A.D. 500). A preoccupation with the liberation of the soul from the bondage of time and matter gave way to the rapt adoration of Brahman in the forms of Vishnu and Shiva. This religion of loving devotion, or *bhakti,* as exemplified in the *Bhagavad Gita* (written c. 100 B.C.-A.D. 100), became the real religion of the masses and has remained so ever since. Mysticism, the identification of the finite with the infinite, did not, however, lead to a renunciation of the world but rather to a hardening of caste lines. For there has always been this double tension within Hindu religion—the striving after liberation from this world (which all Hindus admit to be the final goal of man) on the one hand and

[1] Allan Watts, *Psychotherapy East and West,* Pantheon Books, New York, 1961, p. 9.

[2] *Ibid.,* p. 177.

man's obligation to do what is right in this world on the other. This is the dialectic between *moksha* and *dharma*—liberation and law. And even within *dharma* there is tension between two types of *dharma,* the *sanatana dharma,* or absolute moral order, and the *dharma* of caste and canon law as laid down in such law books as the *Code of Manu* (written c. 200-100 B.C.). Hinduism thus became a social system as well as a religion. Its social framework was the caste system, which with the passing of time became increasingly rigid and complicated (there are more than 3000 castes) and more and more identified with Hinduism as such. By the end of the third phase of Hinduism the pendulum had swung from Vedic polytheism to Upanishadic pantheism and then back again to polytheism; from the "many" to the "One" and back to the "many." How could this have happened? Mysticism, as Paul Tillich observed,

> is the spiritual form of the power of space over time, and therefore we can say that mysticism, in the sense of the great mystics, is the most sublime form of polytheism. In the abyss of the Eternal One, or Atman-Brahman, of the Pure Nothing, of the Nirvana, or whatever the names of this nameless one may be, all individual gods and their spaces disappear. But they only disappear, and therefore they can return. Thus polytheism is the outcome of Hinduism and Brahmanism. But a weakened form; the single gods were not taken quite seriously.[3]

The fourth phase of Hinduism is the present period and is characterized by a denial of the formal self and in its place the reassertion of the self's spiritual essence. This reevaluation of Hinduism came with education and social reform movements in the nineteenth century but spread only among the common people under the aegis of Mahat-

[3] Paul Tillich, *A Theology of Culture,* Oxford University Press, New York, 1959, pp. 34-35.

ma Gandhi (1869-1948). Gandhi believed that man should listen to the voice of this inner self but test its truthfulness through existential acts; truth is discovered by action. Gandhi's ultimacy was "truth force" (*satyagraha*). Truth (*sat*) means simply "what is." Yet, for Gandhi "what is" will depend on one's way of "facing being in all its relativity—relative to an absolute Being who alone is truth, or relative to non-being, or relative to becoming."[4] It is this truth, this "isness," to which one must commit himself in order to experience it as truth. Truth can be found only when one is willing to suffer for it. Or, in the words of Joan Bondurant, Gandhi "transformed absolute truth of the philosophical Sat to the relative truth of ethic principle capable of being tested by means combining non-violent action with self-suffering."[5]

The above is a simplified overview of the development of Hinduism and its core doctrines of ultimate reality and the world. Were these doctrines in fact accepted by the Indian populace? The golden age of classical India, called the Gupta period (c. A.D. 300-500), reveals an emerging dominance of Hinduism over Indian life. By then Hindu philosophy was being expounded and vigorously defended by various orthodox schools—the Vedanta school, the Mimansa school, the Sankhya school, and others. Thus, when Islam arrived in the twelfth century, Hinduism was already the sum and substance of Indian culture. It is not, then, merely a religion within Indian culture; rather Indian culture is the form Hinduism has assumed on the subcontinent.

But what has Hinduism achieved for India in the modern period? Does it have the ideas and symbols for social reform? To answer these questions we must first

[4] Erik Erikson, *Gandhi's Truth,* W. W. Norton and Company, Inc., New York, 1969, p. 413.

[5] *Ibid.,* p. 411.

turn to the sources of India's traditions and ask three questions: (1) What is man? (2) What is his role in society? and (3) What is his life goal?

THE INDIAN MAN

"What is man?" we ask. Classical Hinduism answers something like this: Man is essentially a fragment of divine wholeness or a section of the cloth of nature. Nature embraces both the universe with its fathomless laws and living things. Man does not stand on the threshold of the microcosm and macrocosm as the link between them but is at once a fragment of both. Through the primeval sacrifice of a cosmic being called Purusha and the union of heaven and earth, particularization and identities appeared (*Rig Veda* 6:70), but actually man is but a living thing within the warp and woof of ultimate reality. M. N. Roy put it this way: "The umbilical cord was never broken: man with his mind, intelligence, will, remains an integral part of the physical universe."[6] Hence the Sanskrit words for man—*panin, bhuta, sattva, jiva*—mean simply "living being." This concept is broad enough to cover both material and spiritual extremes. The Jains, India's religious atheists, see life (*jiva*) in all matter—in plants, the elements, water, fire, insects, etc. Shankara (ninth century) pressed this to an all-embracing monism in which man is identified with the impersonal Self of the universe according to the Upanishad formula "That thou art." Vivekananda (nineteenth century) developed the concept into a pantheistic humanism. "So is the relation between god and ourselves. He is in everything. He is everything. Every man and woman is the palpable, blissful, living god."[7]

[6] M. N. Roy, "A New Humanism: A Manifesto," *Sources of the Indian Tradition,* ed. William deBary, Columbia University Press, New York, 1964, II, 362.

[7] From *The Complete Works of Swami Vivekananda,* II, 324-325, quoted in *Sources of the Indian Tradition,* II, 96.

Does man have a soul? The sources answer Yes. In fact, "this soul or *atman* is the real man who transcends the physical, vital, mental and intellectual aspects and has to be identified with the innermost beatific aspect."[8] Man's concern must be directed towards this *atman,* for this is the very essence of his being. The Chandogya Upanishad 8:7-12 states: "The Self, atman, who is free from evil, from old age, free from death, free from grief, free from hunger, free from thirst, whose desire is the Real (*satya*), whose intention is the Real, he should be sought after, he should be desired to be comprehended. He obtains all worlds and all desires, who having found out that Self, knows him."[9] And this *atman* is identical with the ultimate principle of the universe, the neuter Brahman which is "absolute existence, intelligence, and bliss."[10]

"What is the relation of the soul to the body?" Tradition answers, "O to be disembodied!" The body is the unfortunate agent of misery, the fetter binding man to *samsara,* the transmigratory cycle of mortal existence. Thus the Indian dialectic is not over conflicting ideas in man's brain, but between two modes of existence—body and soul. The Jains want to cut this tension by asceticism (*tapas*); self-inflicted pain liberates the *atman* from the tomb-like body. Shankara taught that the body-versus-soul syndrome arises whenever man considers his *atman* a particularized entity apart from the great Self of Brahman.

How to put down this conflict is the concern of Indian religion. The Sankhya system of Kapila strives through knowledge to bring men to see a difference between *atman* and matter. The Yoga system tries to free the self from the world of sensation by physical and noetic disciplines. The

8 deBary, ed., *Sources of the Indian Tradition,* I, 27.

9 *Ibid.,* pp. 28, 29.

10 *Ibid.,* p. 310.

Vedanta school thinks that liberation will come through banishing ignorance:

> The individual soul, which appears different from other souls, and also from Brahman, is in fact nothing but the one unitary Brahman. Since ignorance lies at the root of the seeming duality, knowledge alone is regarded as the means to liberation. Religious actions have only a secondary function in that they may direct the mind to knowledge, but in themselves can never bring about liberation.[11]

The self is perfect. There is no need to cultivate it, only release it. Matter is the focal point of the problem, and it is to this festering mass that man must direct his attention. All is amiss. There is no easy formula for opting out of the body in one blissful moment, for one may have his soul released only to have it enmeshed again in another form of existence—a higher caste possibly, or if one does not behave himself, in an animal. As William deBary says, "The goal of the philosophical quest is liberation from the misery of going from birth to birth and death to death; and the attainment of everlasting bliss. In some cases the everlasting bliss is simply release (mukti or moksha) from the transmigratory cycle (samsara), or the suffering caused by the material enslavement of the spirit."[12] Hence the soul is pushed along its journey away from the body by knowledge, awareness, contemplation, and devotion. The Jains go to a paradoxical extreme; action (*karma*) must be prevented from flowing into the soul and choking its possible release. "The soul can never gain liberation until it has rid itself of its whole accumulation of *karma,* and therefore Jain ascetics subject themselves to rigorous courses of penance and fasting in order to get their souls free of the *karma* already acquired, while all their actions

11 *Ibid.*

12 *Ibid.*, p. 298.

are most carefully regulated to prevent the further influx in serious quantities."[13]

THE INDIAN IN SOCIETY

What is man's role in society? Man is in society for a purpose—liberation. True, there must be society and cultural progress, but the main goal is emancipation of the individual. So what is man's place in society? The answer comes back in the form of a question: How were you born? What is your caste? Through the *samsara* of previous existence, birth and rebirth, a man has progressed (or retrogressed) so far. How he has behaved within his caste will hasten or hinder the liberating process. You must go to the law (*dharma*). It has two ideals: ". . . the organization of social life through well-defined and well-regulated classes (*varnas,* meaning 'color'), and the organization of the individual's life within those classes into definite stages (*ashramas*)."[14] These class divisions were determined in primeval times by man's relation to the communal sacrifice, as *Rig Veda* 10:90 clearly teaches: "His mouth became the *brahman;* his two arms were made into the *rajanya;* his two thighs, the *vaishyas;* from his two feet the *shudra* were born."[15] The *brahmans* became India's priestly class, the communicators between Brahman and society; the *rajanya,* her warrior class, protecting society; the *vaishyas,* her merchant class, nourishing society; the *shudra,* her serfs, serving the other three classes.

Each man within his predetermined class must progress from student of the *dharma* (which underscores his lot in life) to householder, then to hermit, and finally to the ascetic's life, preparing for the final leap out of the cycle. Emphasis throughout the social system is upon negation.

[13] *Ibid.,* p. 47.
[14] *Ibid.,* p. 213.
[15] *Ibid.,* p. 15.

Negativism becomes the ticket to positive release. The Indian sage (*muni*) is one who maintains silence. The yogi keeps five moral precepts: nonviolence (*ahimsa*), sincerity (*satya*), non-theft (*asteya*), chastity (*brahmacarya*), and non-property (*aparigraha*). Three of these are negative. Nakamura Hajime comments: "Thus the Indians are apt to see morality in the negation of the secular human action, so that they lay stress on the negative phase."[16] And because this life is but a barrier to the perfect life—fulfillment in Brahman—there comes a devaluation of science, history, geography, archeology, etc. Sanskrit nouns are abstractions. Differences between subject and object have been blurred. Final truth "exists where all forms of discrimination have been neglected."[17] The principles of logic are of no consequence. Man in his effort to avoid the trammels of this life must view society as a means not an end. The real, the actual, the significant lies beyond the world in which man lives. Thus "there is a tendency among the Indians, divested in general of the concept of a perceptible objective order, not to differentiate too sharply between the actual and the ideal or between fact and imagination or fantasy."[18] Such indifference to society (except in the area of caste) takes a strange twist as the Indian travels down the path of life. By studying Artha Shastra (the science of profit and gain), man may pursue profit "irrespective of the nature of the means."[19] In the organization of the state, the stronger must press his advantage to the fullest. *Kama* (pleasure) can be another legitimate goal, for the pursuit of pleasure is but the soul's express desire for release. Hence the religious man of culture may freely enjoy every sensuous pleasure. As the

16 Nakamura Hajime, *Ways of Thinking of Eastern Peoples,* Japanese National Commission for UNESCO, Tokyo, 1960, p. 106.

17 *Ibid.,* p. 135.

18 *Ibid.,* p. 123.

19 deBary, I, 232.

Song of Tyagaraja expresses it: "O mind! The knowledge of the science and art of music bestows on a person the bliss of oneness with the Supreme Being."[20]

THE INDIAN LIFE GOAL

Though Indian life tends to polarize around *dharma* and *moksha,* law and liberation, *moksha* has the greater attraction. True, *dharma* arranges life into four distinct stages, but each stage, after all, is a progressive disengagement from *dharma.* The real goal is final release of the soul from *samsara.* For man is essentially soul. Unfortunately his soul has been incarcerated in a body. These stages are tangled woods wherein the soul may struggle for release. Society itself, the next generation living in the same poor houses, is of no great concern. One must treat society as a means. Finally one will emerge from the jungle into a clearing—the *moksha.* Here life's goal is reached, here one is absorbed into or finds essential identity with the absolute.[21] Even the personal self of the body perishes with the body. But this is the beginning of the deathless, bodiless impersonal Self.

INDIAN SOCIAL REFORM

Have the above ideas about man and society achieved the kind of life all Indians want? What is the situation in modern India? Percival Spear comments: "The newcomer, fresh from a Western world in ferment and doubt, and hoping here to find wisdom and stability, is shocked to discover that world itself in dissolution and anxiously asking the familiar questions: Whence have we come, whither are we going, why and wherefore?"[22] In seeking

20 *Ibid.,* p. 270.

21 *Ibid.,* p. 272.

22 Percival Spear, *India, Pakistan, and the West,* Oxford University Press, London, 1968, p. 6.

India's wisdom for our modern social problems, we are staggered to find them not solved but multiplied tenfold. The problems specifically are these: (1) poverty—"the crowds on station platforms, the mendicants with quavering voices who stand between the rails below higher class carriages"[23] are symbolic of the ever-widening gulf between rich and poor; (2) poor health—though Western-trained doctors are in the great population centers, absenteeism, epidemics, high death rates, lethargy, and the early onset of old age point to low health standards; (3) unemployment and (4) overpopulation—industrial development is not keeping pace with domestic needs. All these tell the same story—social chaos.

Was Hinduism not accepted by the people? Did she fail to communicate? On the contrary, Hinduism created a cosmological unity, an "ontocracy," a dominion of "what is," or in the words of Arend Van Leeuwen, "a dominance of Pure Essence."[24] Everything, every social institution, was seen to share in this totality of existence, and this totality applied its power to preserve the life and order of society. Hindu temples and their stupas stand as monuments to this central idea—the union of heaven and earth in the person of the cosmic ruler. Every social structure was given a divine dimension—so much so that there could be no critical apparatus standing above the system like a conscience, or an ethic that umpires the societal actions of men. True, the caste system preserved India from internecine warfare in a polyglot society. India's crafts, her trade, her art, were placed in the hands of a set group who lived out their lives within that group. But this system, in the words of Jawaharlal Nehru, developed a "spirit of exclusiveness which sapped the creative faculty and de-

23 *Ibid.*, p. 7.

24 Arend Van Leeuwen, *Christianity and World History*, tr. H. H. Hoskins, Charles Scribner's Sons, New York, 1966, p. 165.

veloped a narrow, small group and parochial outlook."[25] Thus Hinduism like a sacred elephant had the capability of moving at will through large segments of the Indian populations and could have effected social reform and promoted progress. But it was rendered immobile by the ropes of its own system of laws and customs.

At the end of the fourteenth century came the Moguls, the Islamic Mongols, striking swiftly through the northwest (Punjab) and making raids on petty kingdoms. The Mogul, once he had established his divine right to rule by military prowess and cunning, became absolute sovereign to whom was given unfeigned allegiance. From the Koran came authority and encouragement for the "holy war" (*jihad*)—"fight then, until persecution is no more and religion is for Allah." The Islamic social system was essentially theocratic, finding its authority in the Canonical Law of Islam (the *Sharia*)—a comprehensive system of regulations covering every facet of life, whether religious, political, social, domestic, or individual. The Sharia was to dominate the whole gamut of a Muslim's life. But there was "room for wide variation of belief and practice within the ambit of the Holy Law."[26] Authorities paid lip service to the Law and enacted whatever ordinances they wished. Thus we see Islamic rulers behaving in high-handed, capricious ways. During the sixteenth and seventeenth centuries, Akbar, Jahangir, and Shah Jahan built beautiful extravaganzas like the Taj Majal out of tax revenues. Such monuments had little utilitarian value, they impoverished national treasuries, and they set the stage for rebellion. Finally, the Marathas, oppressed lower castes from the Deccan, united under Sivaji (d. 1680) and mounted the attack against the Moguls. As the Moguls

[25] Jawaharlal Nehru, *Toward Freedom: An Autobiography*, The John Day Company, New York, 1941, p. 127.

[26] deBary, I, 398.

reacted harshly to suppress them, India became decentralized, breaking up into a welter of enervated petty states. Then, just as the Mogul sun began to set, the spectre of imperialism appeared from the West. India was totally unprepared to meet this challenge.

Actually, while the Moguls were at the zenith of their power, Western forces were already at India's doors. The British, Dutch, Portuguese, French, and Danes came seeking their fortunes in the East during the sixteenth and seventeenth centuries. Britain, shut out of the spice trade in Java by the Dutch, had to content herself with less lucrative trade with India. But India was torn by internecine warfare, and as the East India Company tried to achieve political stability through allegiances with promising rajahs, Britain moved reluctantly from commerce to politics. The Marathas, after losing the decisive Battle of Paniput with the Afghans in 1761, became greatly weakened and could not unify the country. Britain moved to fill the political vacuum and found herself the inheritor of a vast continent overnight. But observing the debacle of the Portuguese in Goa, who became entangled in Indian customs, the British adopted a policy of noninvolvement with Indian society.

Thus we see three great forces striding through Indian society on the eve of the modern period—Hinduism, Islam, and British imperialism—all wielding great power but all of them unconcerned with social reform.

Buddhism is indigenous to India but cannot be considered a major force there, since it enjoyed only limited acceptance by the people. It was, however, a critique of Hindu culture. The founder of Buddhism, Siddhartha Gautama (c. 550-460 B.C.), was a young prince of the Sakya tribe in the Himalayan hills. Had it not been for a casual chariot drive beyond the palace walls at the age of twenty-nine, Siddhartha would have remained content within his warrior caste. What he saw everywhere shocked him. Life for common man, caught within the endless cycle of *samsara,* was unbearably hard—full of sorrow, suffering, and death. But a chance encounter with a religious ascetic who evidenced great composure amidst such suffering affected Siddhartha deeply. He abandoned palace life and sought *moksha* by living first as a beggar, then as a forest hermit. But six years of rigorous striving for liberation in Indian forests were of no avail. He began to seriously question the Hindu solution to man's basic problem. Finally, under a pipal tree in the town of Gaya in Bihar province, Siddhartha became "enlightened," that is, he attained Buddhahood. Tradition tells us that the Buddha delivered his first sermon at a deer park in Benares. In this sermon he enumerated the Four Noble Truths of Buddhism, namely that life is full of sorrow, that sorrow stems from man's craving for personal satisfaction, that sorrow can be stopped if man will abandon his craving, and that craving or thirst can be stopped if man will pursue a middle course between asceticism and self-indulgence, a course that is essentially a disciplined, moral life. Interpreters of Buddhism agree that it is more a psychology than a religion; its goal is a change of consciousness in the individual, a new awareness of himself and the world. For the enlightened, the social structures of the world become one grand illusion. Thus caste—the basic structure of Indian society—is mere social conditioning from which man must seek release. *Moksha* or *nirvana* (the de-spirited place or state where personality vanishes) is found not by making a long, arduous journey through the four stages of Hindu life, but by treating *samsara* as an illusion, the "endlessly repetitious attempt to solve a false problem."[27] Emancipation is not release of soul from body but of self from social institutions. And this is

27 Watts, p. 17.

accomplished by seeing the self as an illusory concept, the projection of society's values upon the individual. The caste system can be ignored, for there is not a separate ego to perpetuate it. In summary, Buddhism is a psychological attempt to unite being with nonbeing, subject with object, life with death; it is an attempt to detach the self from socially imposed norms and allow it to become part of the universal self, not acting, not choosing, not striving, but caught up within the great rhythm of the phenomenal world. Thus Buddhism brought release from man's human predicament and encouraged a life without attachment to the world. *Samsara* also disappeared with the ego. As Watts suggests, "The anxiety of endless migration came to an end with the realization that there is no one to endure it."[28] But because of Buddhism's concept of ultimate reality—the void or relativity (*sunyata*)—it could be syncretistic and tolerate Hindu practices. With the resurgence of Hinduism in the ninth century (under the aegis of Shankara), Buddhism became assimilated into Hinduism. Buddha himself came to be considered the tenth incarnation of Vishnu. Thus, along with Hinduism it came under devastating attack by the Moguls and retreated to Nepal and Tibet. The Buddhist struggle against caste was over.

Sikhism, a small religious movement in northwest India founded by Nanak (1469 1539), attempted to reconcile the best elements of Hinduism and Islam into one syncretistic system. The Sikhs broke caste, repudiated empty ritual, deplored meaningless asceticism, maintained equality of the sexes, and affirmed an ethical, disciplined life. Thus Sikhism was originally a quasi-social reform movement. The political chaos of the Mogul period, however, diverted the movement into a military theocracy, fighting for its life within a hostile Muslim environment. But that is not the whole reason for its departure from social reform.

28 *Ibid.*, p. 65.

The Sikh experiment demonstrated that syncretism is simply not a viable modus operandi for generating social reform; it diverts energy toward reconciling not reforming elements in society. From where, then, did social reform come? Percival Spear traces the beginnings of active social welfare in India back to two British streams of thought—utilitarianism and evangelicalism:

> These two movements formed intellectual pressure groups for reform and interference in India along Western lines. They were, each in their own ways westernizing influences, tending to replace Indian customs, values, and ways of thought by European. They did not control the government of India, but their influence ensured that when the government moved at all, it would move along the lines which they laid down.[29]

The utilitarians, as represented by William Bentinck, Lord Macaulay, and J. S. Mill (who spent his working life in the London India house) brought about the abolition of widow burning (*sati*) in 1828, and in 1835 the abolition of unjust transit duties and the introduction of English as the language of education. It was Macaulay and his famous "Minute on Education" that brought the content of learning to practical studies, turning Indian minds away from Hindu classics and antiquities. This brought about a linguistic revolution, threatening the whole Hindu-Islamic intellectual structure. It also had a profound influence upon social and political events. "The older elites were gradually replaced by a new class of Indians trained in a foreign language and a foreign culture, able to act as intermediaries between the British and the bulk of the people."[30] These Indians dropped their fervent attachment to religious traditions. They "broke out of the mold of caste and custom [and] embraced Western ideas and standards of behavior. [These new Indians] were Indian in

29 Spear, p. 101.
30 deBary, II, 36, 37.

blood and color, but English in taste, in opinions, in morals and in intellect."[31] English became the lingua franca of the educated Indian world, and this new language unified a country hitherto divided by regional languages. The English language served as a catalyst for political self-consciousness and Indian nationalism.

But the work of the utilitarians had to be augmented by the work of the evangelicals, for in the words of Spear, the overemphasis on utilitarianism in education "blighted the prospect of intellectual renaissance."[32] It was the Christian missionaries who restored balance with their emphasis upon liberal arts. "The first Christian Arts college, apart from Danish Serampore, was the Scottish Churches College founded by Alexander Duff in 1835, and soon India was covered with a network of Christian institutions within the official framework."[33] Who were these evangelicals? Many of them were Christians within the East India Company. Charles Grant, for example, as Chairman of the Company, influenced the foreign personnel and the surrounding Indian communities in morals and outlook. Whenever universal moral law was flouted in Indian life, these men took issue, suppressing such practices as child sacrifice and robbery involving ritual murder (*thagi*). The English idea of man's equality before law, though not rigidly upheld when Englishmen stood to lose, gradually affected Indian jurisprudence. For centuries the application of Hindu law had been influenced by caste. Also, during the period of the Moguls, laws favoring Muslims over Hindus had been enacted. Hence the concept of equality before law was revolutionary. By 1832 the Hindu law of inheritance was modified "by a regulation allowing those who changed their religion to retain their property."[34] Another breach

31 *Ibid.*, p. 37.

32 Spear, p. 105.

33 *Ibid.*, pp. 105-106.

34 *Ibid.*, p. 107.

of orthodox Hindu custom came with the 1856 Widow Remarriage Act, allowing Hindu widows to retain their rights upon remarriage. Medical institutions founded by Christian missions quickly outpaced Hindu and Muslim medical facilities, both hopelessly medieval and bordering on quackery. Thus went the work of social reform within the framework of the East India Company, through the aegis of Christian men like Wilberforce, Shaftesbury, Grant, and Brown.

Standing outside any legal framework, Protestant missionaries also worked indefatigably towards social reform. The efforts of the English Baptists William Carey, Joshua Marshman, and William Ward were not meant to demonstrate a victory of Christian ideas over Hindu tradition. These men wished to promote human happiness. Nor were their frequent articles in the *Friend of India* quarterly describing "certain dreadful practices" written by detached scholars bent on denigrating religious opponents. What they encountered in early nineteenth-century India drove them to action; the quarterly served indirectly as a lobby to British parliament, urging legal action for the betterment of Indian society.

Four areas in which missionaries worked for reform were caste, religious freedom, education, and child laws. Let us briefly consider them. I have already mentioned how the institution of caste was challenged by Buddha himself. His followers furthered the struggle by bringing men from all walks of life together in a common monastic life. Sikhs made a frontal attack on caste by having initiates eat from a common bowl (*Sikh* means "bowl") and by adopting the common surname Singh, thereby eliminating social distinctions based on family name. Carey, Marshman, and Ward believed that caste was a "prison far stronger than any which the civil tyrannies of the world have ever erected; a prison which immures many millions of innocent beings."[35] By permitting converts to marry across caste lines, the Baptists scandalized Hindu society. This all but insured a rejection of their message by the higher castes. Thus unwittingly they and their followers found themselves bringing to birth a new caste—a Christian caste. Later missionaries took different approaches to the problem. Some accepted caste as a social fact of India as they did the social strata in England. They feared that a frontal attack would lead to social anarchy. Some educational missionaries attempted to establish schools where caste was not observed, but discovered that intelligent Hindu youth avoided the schools for that reason. So these educators set up different schools—for the pariahs or outcastes who had become Christians and for the Hindu youth who were not Christian and for whom caste was the issue. In some schools like the Serampore Mission College in the Danish sector, caste was not observed. One missionary, William Howell, set up looms in a factory and established his own community of Christians. However, the number of missionaries working against caste was relatively small; their greatest influence was more by instruction and example. Such example nourished a critical approach to caste among the Indian population. By 1850 the concept that education should be above caste was finding theoretical acceptance among Hindu intellectuals. An attempt to cashier the Indian educator Bose in 1848 on the grounds that he was a Christian teaching Hindu students was thwarted by the government.

The Baptists also wrote articles in the *Friend of India* against *sati,* the self-immolation of the widow on her husband's funeral pyre. In 1816 the first major pamphlet on the subject was published in England. The author, William Johns, relied heavily on William Ward's second

[35] E. Daniel Potts, *British Baptist Missionaries in India, 1793-1837,* Cambridge University Press, 1967, p. 158.

edition of *Hindoos* for the gruesome details of *sati* practices. To those who maintained that the custom had the approval of religious tradition, Marshman countered in an essay that

> With almost as much justice might the Slave Trade have been regarded with veneration, as a sacred relic of antiquity handed down from the earliest ages;—or the practice of killing all prisoners taken in war;—or that of sacrificing hecatombs of men at the funeral of a favourite chief;—or the conduct of certain banditti [thugs] in this country, who [from time immemorial no doubt] are said to seize men and immolate them at the shrine of their imagined deity.[36]

Bentinck finally made widow burning a criminal offense by his regulation of December 4, 1829. The custom gradually faded out.

The missionaries continued to apply pressure through Christians within the East India Company to abolish the "temple tax," which was a British connivance of state support for temples and shrines. The Company's involvement with Hindu festivals was a continuation of the precedent set by wealthy Indian princes. These princes had contributed to and actually supervised religious pilgrimages. The Company did it ostensibly to foster good relations but actually to placate the people and protect them during these emotion-wrought occasions. But the Baptists took up the pen against festival excesses, for example, "the acts of immolation of the pilgrims who threw themselves to their death under the enormous wheels of the idols' cars."[37] Under constant harassment, the Company in 1833 officially dissociated itself from religious rites inimical to the "spirit of Christianity." These general instructions from the Board of Directors were not, however, carried out. Governor-General Bentinck continued to col-

36 *Ibid.*, p. 150.

37 Kenneth Ingham, *Reformers in India*, Cambridge University Press, 1956, p. 35.

lect the temple tax and to use the revenues for maintaining social services. The missionaries pressed their attack. In 1850, thirty-seven missionaries signed a memorial to the government urging them to check

> the vice, suffering, loss of life and other evils at Jagannath [temple in Bengal] by discontinuing altogether a support so inconsistent with reason, humanity, and religion and which contributes in no slight degree to the misery, temporal and eternal, of the people whom providence has entrusted to your charge; and whose welfare your Honorable Court is bound by every means in your power to promote.[38]

Finally in 1856 the government severed official connection with Jagannath, presaging an ever-widening gulf between church and state.

Legislation works speedy external reform, but the missionaries soon realized that it takes education to produce internal reform. At first the British government took a laissez-faire attitude toward Indian rural education. Only a small proportion of the population were receiving elementary education. "The peasants from poverty and the casual labourers from indifference seldom if ever sent their children to school."[39] Advanced learning was no better. When William Mill visited the Hindu College of Poona in 1822, "he found the level of instruction there very low, and the elementary knowledge which was all that even the professors possessed had produced in them merely mental confusion."[40] In 1781, Jonathan Duncan had founded the Benares Sanskrit College and Warren Hastings a college named the Madrassa. Following traditional lines, neither of these colleges was fulfilling hopes. Fort Williams College, founded in 1800 by Marquis Wellesley, was administered by the Company, with evangelical chaplains and mission-

38 Potts, pp. 166-167.
39 Ingham, p. 56.
40 *Ibid.*, p. 56.

aries like Carey serving on the faculty. But gradually missionaries began founding schools of their own for neglected Eurasians and pariah castes. By 1819 the Baptists had over 7,000 pupils in their schools. By 1824 over 50,000 Indian children were being trained in various mission-related schools. And by 1852, mission-related schools in the field of teacher-training had four times the number of students as did government-sponsored schools. These educational efforts, if not evangelistically rewarding, did at least establish a more detached, critical stance toward life, culture, and religion among Indian students, the first step toward reform from within.

Missionaries also worked to alleviate the suffering of India's children. In 1794 Carey came upon a case of deliberate child exposure and reported it. And in 1802, under the encouragement of Governor-General Wellesley, Carey began investigating alleged cases of infanticide on the island of Saugor near the mouth of the Ganges. Eventually Carey submitted a memorial on "murders committed under the pretence of religion (including sati) in the hope that they would be declared criminal acts. This was not to be, although Regulation VI of 1802 passed by Wellesley did outlaw infanticide at Saugor and elsewhere in Bengal."[41]

In the twentieth century, Irish missionary Amy Carmichael made inroads into an entrenched Indian custom, that of babies and young girls being "dedicated to the gods" and trained for a life of legalized prostitution within the temples. In 1901, a little girl being so trained, but determined to evade that which she scarcely understood, escaped to the temporary home of the missionary and a group of itinerant South Indian women evangelists. They took the little girl, named Preena, in and heard her tell of all she had seen in the temple. For a number of years these

41 Potts, p. 140.

brave women gathered the facts about the temple children. Amy Carmichael would stain her hands and arms with coffee, and dressed in an Indian sari, she and Ponnammal, her constant companion, visited places no foreign woman had ever been:

> Once we stayed in a hostel for priests and pilgrims, and sitting on the floor in the evenings round the brass lamp set on the floor, while a garland maker made garlands for the gods, we listened to the talk, and here and there picked up a clue. Once we slept in a byre (the cow was away), and heard conversation through the wall of the next house, for the wall was thin and the voices loud. This led straight to a child in danger, and also opened our eyes to one of the sources for which we were searching. The child was saved.[42]

The missionary's biographer wrote,

> There lies before me a note-book in which, beginning with the story of Preena, Amma [Amy Carmichael] set down the concrete evidence of the existence of this evil traffic as it gradually accumulated. Omitting a good deal which she felt to be unprintable, she published some of the facts. . . . Incredulity in Mission as well as in Government circles gradually gave place to concern and, in the case of many officials, both Indian and European, to a determination to strengthen the law against the sale of children for immoral purposes. As a result not only of Amma's work but also of the efforts of a great body of reformers it has now been made illegal to dedicate a young child to a god.[43]

In 1919 the British Government honored Amy Carmichael by including her in the Royal Birthday Honours List. She reluctantly accepted the Kaiser-i-Hind Medal for her services to the people of India, but could not be persuaded to go to Madras for the presentation ceremony because "It

42 Quoted by Frank Houghton in *Amy Carmichael of Dohnavur,* SPCK, London, 1953, p. 118.

43 *Ibid.,* p. 116.

troubles me to have an experience so different from His Who was despised and rejected–not kindly honoured."[44]

By the time of her death in 1951, close to 1000 people made up the Dohnavur Fellowship, as the work begun by Amy Carmichael came to be called. In describing this work, she wrote,

> From the first we thought of the children as our own. We did not make a Home for them, when they came to us they were at home. And so from the beginning we were a family, never an institution; and we all, Indian and European, men and women, live and work together on the lines of an Indian family, each contributing what each has to offer for the help of all. We have no salaried workers, Indian or foreign. We have no workers who are only preachers . . . the evangelist shares in the practical work of life–doctoring, nursing, teaching, building, engineering, farming, and so on.[45]

From the day she set foot in India, November 9, 1895, until her death more than fifty-five years later, Amy Carmichael remained in India, and she loved it as few have done. And through her many books, the children of South India became known and loved by people worldwide. The principles by which the Dohnavur Fellowship carried out the missionary task have been esteemed and emulated by missionaries in every part of the globe. She would not have considered herself a "reformer," but she reformed both Indian society and missionary methods.

These missionaries were motivated by a transcendental vision of Indians joining the company of redeemed in heaven. But they were not ignorant of the temporal blessings and enrichment in life that Christianity brings. Ingham sums up their impact for social reform:

> The arrival of the Protestant missionaries in Bengal and southern India after 1793, however, drew new attention to mis-

44 *Ibid.*, p. 195.

45 Amy Carmichael, *Figures of the True*, SPCK, London, 1938, p. 21.

> sionary work in all its forms. The zeal of these men, the diversity of their talents, and the rapid expansion of their sphere of activity had not been equalled since the earliest days of the Jesuits in India. Thousands of Indians, both Hindus and Muslims, felt for the first time the impact of enthusiastic evangelism inseparably bound up with a programme of social and educational reform. This new activity had a profound effect on those who felt its impulse.[46]

These efforts toward social reform were accelerated by such indigenous Indian movements as Seva Sadan, Harijan Sevak Sangh, and the Indian National Congress, all of which worked for legislative reforms in caste, widow remarriage, and child marriage. The first sentiment for Indian independence came from a brilliant Anglo-Indian educator, Henry Derozio (1809-1831).

> Derozio was raised a Protestant and received the best education available in Calcutta. Nevertheless, his part-Indian ancestry meant he could not hold a responsible government post. Finding office work for his father distasteful, he turned for a living to his uncle's indigo factory in the country. There on the banks of the Ganges River, he composed romantic poems, whose publication made him the talk of Calcutta at seventeen. Two years later he was appointed assistant headmaster at the famous Hindu College, where the brightest young Bengalis were flocking to learn the new knowledge from the West.[47]

Derozio fired the imagination of India's youth and his writings represent the first echo in India of Western ideas and attitudes. Other Indians, like Ananda Pillai (1709-1761), found employment within the Western system, admired what they saw, and benefited economically by Western ideas. Their interest, however, stopped at this point. The dominance of pure essence arrested any thought of reform in Indian society. But Derozio's mind was imbued with Christian idealism. "His verse carried the

46 Ingham, p. 16.
47 deBary, II, 13.

flavor of English romantic poets, and the sentiments he expresses remind us of theirs. His poems to India are virtually the first expressions of Indian nationalist thought, and their appearance among other poetry, dramatizes the fact that modern nationalism is essentially an alien importation into the Indian world of ideas."[48] Another Indian voice for social reform was that of Rāmmohun Roy (1772-1833), called the Father of Modern India. Though Roy did not accept the theological aspects of Christianity, he felt that its humanitarian message was needed by India. He engaged in theological debate with missionaries on the one hand, but despised idolatry and advocated monotheism on the other. "I feel persuaded," he said, "that by separating from the other matters contained in the New Testament, the moral precepts found in that book, these will be more likely to produce the desirable effect of improving the hearts and minds of men of different persuasions and degrees of understanding."[49] Concerning the Christian ethic and its relevance to Indian social reform, he wrote:

> This simple code of religion and morality is so admirably calculated to elevate men's ideas to high and liberal notions of one God, who has equally subjected all living creatures, without distinction of caste, rank, or wealth, to change, disappointment, pain, and death, and has equally admitted all to be partakers of the bountiful mercies which he has lavished over nature, and is also so well fitted to regulate the conduct of the human race in the discharge of their various duties to God, to themselves, and to society, that I cannot but hope the best effects from its promulgation in the present form.[50]

Lastly, we must discuss Mahatma Gandhi (1869-1948), father of Indian independence, pioneer in militant nonviolence, and model for Martin Luther King. Gandhi's

48 *Ibid.*, p. 14.
49 *Ibid.*, p. 25.
50 *Ibid.*

eclectic religious and ethical beliefs grew out of a background in Vaishnavite Hinduism, an acquaintance with the Jains and their teachings on *ahimsa* (nonviolence to all creatures), and a knowledge of Christianity gained in London and South Africa. He sailed to England at the age of eighteen and during his three years of studying in London heard some of England's greatest preachers. But, though Newman's "Lead kindly light . . . one step enough for me" became his favorite hymn and the Sermon on the Mount went straight to his heart, Gandhi never professed conversion to Christianity. He was scandalized later by racial prejudices in South Africa. But what most hindered his adoption of Christianity was the persistent Hindu view that everyone shares in a divine essence; he could not accept Christ's uniqueness. Yet, he did borrow from Christian ethics. Tolstoy's *The Kingdom of God Is Within You* "overwhelmed him with its message of Christian pacifism. . . . His studies of the Sermon on the Mount and the *Gita* led him to the conclusion that the ideal life was one of selfless action in the service of one's fellow men, and the best method of righting wrongs was to protest nonviolently and to suffer lovingly rather than submit to injustice."[51] To suffer for a cause and discover truth in that suffering was Gandhi's way of inspiring hope among India's oppressed masses. With his concept of "soul force" (*satyagraha,* meaning truth-insistence) Gandhi went to jail repeatedly rather than obey unjust laws. "He took seriously the New Testament injunction to return good for evil, and often referred to Jesus as the Prince of Civil Resisters."[52] His indefatigable efforts in ethical politics finally achieved Indian independence in 1947.

51 *Ibid.,* p. 248.
52 *Ibid.,* p. 250.

2

China

In traditional Chinese thinking, a cosmic order dominates the world. This rational order is diffused in nature but also governs human relationships. Chinese society ideally is a replica of a heavenly hierarchy; the harmony of the universe can and should be reflected among men. Like stars in their courses men achieve accord on earth by proper role playing in every sector of life. This concept has affected Chinese thinking on man, society and life goals from Confucius to Mao Tse-tung.

But isn't the Communism of Mao Tse-tung and the Cultural Revolution a repudiation of this notion? History, says Mao, is characterized by class struggle—from slavery to feudalism, feudalism to imperialistic capitalism, and capitalism to Communism. China's history affords clear proof that this historical theory is correct. But what of Confucianism, Taoism, Buddhism, and Neo-Confucianism, those philosophical concepts that shaped China's culture and her views about man? True, these schools of thought have been rejected by Chinese Communist scholars ever since the May 4th Movement of 1919. However, bringing 700 million people within the Communist ideological orbit could not have been achieved simply by importing a politico-economic theory from the West. Marxism has been sinicized on Chinese soil. It has been presented through the medium of the Chinese language and in the milieu of a culture permeated with ideas about man and his destiny, ideas crystallized from Confucianism, Taoism, and Neo-Confucianism.

Communist scholars will be quick to dip into these traditions to illustrate essential Marxist ideas—for example, Confucius' agnosticism, materialism, and concern for social reform; Mencius' equal-fields system; the legalistic measures of the Chin to abolish feudalism and set the stage for a bureaucracy; the "mandate" of the Party; Chu Hsi's immutable principle of the *li,* which makes Marxism not merely a Western idea transplanted to Chinese soil but a universal truth. Such compatible ideas will be kept to illustrate the historical class struggle and modern China's indebtedness to her ancient proletariat. On the other hand, traditional ideas of decorum, timeless morality, conservatism, heaven, filial piety, the Five Relationships—all these will be ruthlessly excoriated and banished from official doctrine. Yet, to understand how the Chinese man was able to slough off this time-worn Confucian garment for a Marxist one, or better, to recognize some of the old patterns and threads remaining in the new garment, we must examine closely China's cultural past.

First, to discover sources of ultimacy in Chinese thinking we leave the Communist politburo and visit a thriving, well-organized Chinese commune. There we will notice at the workers' confabs, women's meetings, and student forums, the ubiquitous red Bible of modern China—*Quotations from Chairman Mao.* Unlike the Confucian Classics which when mastered gave status to an elite minority, the *Quotations* are known by all and directed toward fulfillment of the masses. Actually they are the distillation of "mass-thought" expressed concisely by Mao. But what of religious ultimacy and pervasive concerns? Is there a qualitative difference in emphasis between the Classics and Mao? We notice some continuity. Both present a consistent humanism. Not metaphysics, not escape, not flight into the beyond, but the concrete, the here and now, man standing between heaven and earth—these have been the concern of Chinese thought from earliest times to the present. Religious ultimacy then as now was immanent, within nature. Even the term "heaven" (*t'ien*) referred to cultural heroes like the Yaos and the Shuns who inhabit heaven. They were once men who achieved moral perfection on earth through right conduct, decorum, and propriety. Man in the Chinese scheme of things has always been the earth around which ideas orbit. Metaphysical speculation has always been irrelevant. But every agrarian system, every legal system, every scheme of taxation devised to effect a humanistic utopia ran aground on the unseen reefs of human nature. So charting human nature was a must for Chinese philosophies, and our question "What is man?" is none other than that which has been asked by Chinese minds since antiquity.

THE CHINESE MAN

Before Confucius, from the Shang through the Western Chou (1766-770 B.C.) periods, human nature was considered a gift from heaven invested with heaven's moral order. Sinologists have pieced together China's earliest known culture from oracle "dragon" bones discovered at Anyang and ancient bronzes cast to commemorate epochal achievements. It was an agrarian society with highly artistic sculptures and ideographic writing. The family system was so strong in this period that obligations to one's parent continued after his decease. The Shang people believed that man's spirit lingers after death among the living, performing malevolent or benevolent acts upon them.

Hence the expiatory sacrifice was important. In fact the Shang people seemed more concerned with the dead than the living, for they did not solve life's problems by a council of elders but rather by a council of the deceased, whose ideas and directives could be ascertained by technical divination rites on the shoulder bones of cows or tortoise shells. Life was cheap during the Shang period. People were kept in abject slavery, buried alive with petty kings, even offered as sacrifices to appease the ancestors. Heaven was the abode of these ancestors. Greatest ancestor of them all was Shang-ti (highest emperor), legendary moral governor of the universe, perfectly righteous, imparting wisdom to those earthly sovereigns who conduct prescribed rituals scrupulously and walk uprightly. Animal sacrifices kept open the lines of communication to heaven. During the Western Chou period, the Mandate of Heaven (*t'ien-ming*) concept grew into an important political expedient. The Chou dukes who overthrew the sophisticated Shang were rustics from the West. The Mandate of Heaven concept gave a mantle of legitimacy to their dynasty, saying in effect that rulers are appointed by heaven for governing in the best interests of the governed. A ruler, then, may legitimately rule as long as he does so in the people's interest. Heaven chooses the ruler and the man to replace him. Summarizing, during China's earliest dynasties there were incipient ideas which said that there is in man something morally good through which heaven can effect its will upon earth.

The Eastern Chou period (770-221 B.C.) was one of chaos and anarchy. The dynastic family ruled in name only and were removed to the eastern capital at Loyang, away from marauding hordes from the west. During this period the major philosophical schools arose, each presenting ideas about the world, government, society and man. Confucius (560-480 B.C.), archetype of the literati school (*ju*), believed that human nature could be improved by learning and ethical action. His teachings and the teaching of those following in the *ju* tradition have given an indelible humanistic stamp to Chinese philosophy. He said, "In their original natures men closely resemble each other; in their acquired practices, they grow wide apart."[1] Accretions of ignorance, impropriety, and selfishness must be swept away by discipline and decorum. True humanity is achieved through learning. Man must return to the ways of the cultural heroes—the Yaos, the Shuns, and the Duke Chou. Through ceremonial rites and proper decorum man may range himself on the side of goodness (*jen*). Waley defines *jen* as a "sublime moral attitude, a transcendental perfection attained by legendary figures."[2] The driving force enabling man to side with *jen* is *te*—moral power. This goodness seems not so much uprightness as a careful maintenance of right relationships. Mencius (372-298 B.C.) took this incipient humanism to an extreme. Man, he said, has not merely a capacity for goodness, but has innately such qualities as sympathy, justice, and love. Doing what comes naturally will be doing the good. It could not be otherwise. Doing evil is a deliberate suppression of one's upward yearning to do the good. Mo-tzu's teachings (470-391 B.C.) were considered a threat to the Confucian tradition, but actually followed in the same humanistic, optimistic vein. He said that all men are equal before heaven. To follow heaven is to practice love for all men. Morality and law must be practiced to procure the greatest happiness for the greatest number. Communist egalitarianism is nothing new to Chinese minds schooled in Mo-tzu's writings.

On the other end of the spectrum, Hsün-tzu (d. 238 B.C.), Han-fei-tzu (d. 233 B.C.), and the Legalist School (*fa*

[1] *Sources of the Chinese Tradition,* ed. William deBary, Columbia University Press, New York, 1964, I, 23.

[2] Arthur Waley, *The Analects of Confucius,* Random House, New York, 1938, p. 28.

chia) were unimpressed with the harvest society was reaping from such psychological optimism. Hsün-tzu asked three questions of his Confucian peers: If man is essentially good, (1) why does evil come easily but good remain elusive; (2) why are social conditions so deplorable; (3) what is the rationale for laws and rulers to hold man in check? His own thesis was this: "The nature of man is evil; his goodness is acquired."[3] This followed his first premise, that heaven is impersonal and amoral. Since heaven is mechanistic and lacks ethical principles, it follows that man's nature, derived from this heaven, is also devoid of inherent ethical goodness. Goodness must be superimposed upon man; only a detailed system of laws and punishments can curb man's proclivity toward evil. He put it this way: "Crooked wood needs to undergo steaming and bending by the carpenter's tools; then only is it straight. Blunt metal needs to undergo grinding and whetting; then only is it sharp. Now the original nature of man is evil, so he must submit himself to teachers and laws before he can be just."[4]

The Confucianists were preoccupied with a cosmic order; man's laws should reflect this order. But the Legalists were preoccupied with society; laws should define the right. These laws enable society to run smoothly and are not mere reflections of a cosmic *Tao.* Legalist philosophy triumphed during the Chin dynasty (221-206 B.C.), enabling terrorist totalitarianism, harsh laws, and cruel punishments to unite China for the first time (and incidentally complete the 1400-mile-long Great Wall). Confucian scholars of later dynasties castigated Chin repressiveness, but realistically never abandoned its legalist procedures. For the system of legal codes born of this pessimistic view of man actually created just the stability

[3] deBary, I, 104.

[4] *Ibid.*

needed to realize the Confucian bureaucratic ideal. Hence, modern China's surrender of individual freedom to the authoritarianism of the Communist Party so that the masses might resolutely shake off the fetters of capitalism and usher in the classless society—such a modus operandi is as old as China's first dynasty. In the words of Edwin O. Reischauer, "One could say that the Legalist spirit is more obviously alive in Communist China today than either Confucian morality or Taoistic nature-mysticism."[5]

But the Chinese are lovers of freedom. Thus it is not surprising that a passive resistance movement to the Confucian social structure developed through the centuries. Many Chinese thinkers considered Confucianism's meticulous rules of decorum a threat to free expression and the enjoyment of life itself. They first were taken up with nature and her effortless way. The latter they called Tao—nameless, formless, nonbeing; it cannot be heard, it cannot be seen, it cannot be spoken. Man, according to the Taoists, has within him a spark of the Tao. He should be free to conform to the Tao, to express himself in the way of the Tao—unhindered, unfettered, doing what comes naturally. The way of the Confucian was within the mold of society, a society shaped by custom and ritual; the way of the Taoist was the way of the universe. The Taoist movement was in essence an ancient hippie movement—the recourse of frustrated scholars fed up with society and retreating to the forest or the mountains to merge with nature, write poetry, paint, drink, revel. Ideal man to the Taoist could not be found in society. How could he be? The perfect man was the unborn child, the uncarved block. To find one's pristine self, one had to cast away man-made, man-imposed social inhibitions. One famous Taoist kept with him at all times an attendant holding a bottle of rice wine in one hand and a spade in the other. The wine

[5] Edwin Reischauer and John Fairbank, *East Asia: The Great Tradition*, Houghton Mifflin Company, Boston, 1960, p. 84.

he proffered his master when thirst overtook him, the spade he held in readiness in case death should overtake him. These Taoists encouraged the disillusioned upper classes to withdraw from society during times of chaos. They even inveigled some emperors who sought immortality to take "trips" via their potent elixirs. It is Taoism that gave birth to Chinese alchemy, cuisine, impressionist art, and inner hygiene (the prolongation of life by breathing exercises). The Taoist is to walk in the nameless path of the universe. Evil is not going against an established norm like law but is a falling away from the harmonious centrality of the universe. Thus, the Taoist doctrine of the relativity of human values could well serve Communist ideology as the psychological preparation for casting aside cultural patterns and historical precedent.

Taoist, Buddhist, and Confucian ideas were woven together into one philosophical garment by Neo-Confucian scholars of the Sung dynasty (A.D. 960-1279). They did it with a Chinese character called *li* (理), first mentioned in the *Classic of Changes.* How did they do this? That there is an unseen, unifying principle in the universe has been a recurrent theme of philosophy. Greeks called it the *logos;* Indians, the *dharma;* Buddhists, the *sunyata;* Neo-Confucianists, the *li.* This concept of the *li*—the organizing principle of the universe—also shaped Confucian ideas of man. By the time of the Sung dynasty, Buddhism, rocked by the great persecutions of A.D. 841-845, had passed its apogee and was declining in influence. Confucianism had been enervated by both Buddhism and Taoism but kept very much alive by the examination system. The Neo-Confucians, rejecting Taoism as anti-political and Buddhism as anti-social, hoped to recapture the original vision of benevolent government through an efficient bureaucracy. But Confucianism had been bound by earth; it needed a metaphysical dimension to give it religious status along with Taoism and Buddhism. It fell to Neo-Confucianists like Chou-Tun-i (A.D. 1012-1073), Ch'eng Hao (A.D. 1031-1085), Ch'eng I (A.D. 1032-1107), and Chu Hsi (A.D. 1130-1200) to formulate a new system of thought, borrowing from existing philosophies and traditional Confucian ideals. Chu Hsi, who gave final expression to this new Confucianism, had grown up in a Buddhist monastery and studied Taoism. The Taoist way and the Buddhist void attracted him, but these concepts lifted man out of earth's plane. Chu Hsi said that all things—nature, society, man—had their organizing principle, and that this *li* could be discovered through an investigation of things. *Li* in itself is invisible but could be discovered through *chi*—vital energy or substance. This is similar to the Western concepts of natural law and matter. A leaf and a flower may have the same *chi* but are different because governed by a different *li*, the *li* of flowerness as opposed to the *li* of leafness. The *li* raised to cosmic proportions was the *T'ai-chi* or Great Ultimate. T'ai-chi was the sum of the *li*, indivisible in nature. As the moon is one, though reflected in 10,000 streams, so the *li* is an entity though diffused in nature. The Neo-Confucianists took this concept into the realm of psychology, calling man's nature also the *li*, or better, a participator in the *li* of the universe. And this metaphysical *li* did not remove man from society; on the contrary it was this *li* that enabled man to walk in accord with the universe during his life on earth. Wing-tsit Chan comments: "Man's sense of order and value does not alienate him from the universe but is precisely what unites him to it. The world of human ethics, of social relations, of history and political endeavor is a real one, not just a passing dream or nightmare from which man must be awakened, as the Buddhist said, to the truth of emptiness."[6] The *li* governs human relationships. As the source of the five Confucian virtues—human-heartedness, righteousness, propriety, wis-

6 deBary, I, 456.

dom, and sincerity–it determines the character of man's acts as well as natural phenomena. The *li* is invisible until manifested through *ch'i*–ethereal matter–which for man becomes his peculiar natural endowment. Moral law, then, is the human application of the laws of nature, immutable and binding like all her laws. Chu Hsi was a rationalist, departing from the Confucian sages who held that morals and ethics were determined by a moral administrator of the universe (Shang-ti). In his words, "Heaven contains no sovereign . . . [though] on the other hand, it cannot be said that the earth is without a master, since it is governed by the *li*."[7] But as Rene Grousset observes, "This motive power of the world is not to be thought of as a universal consciousness, an ineffable spirituality, the soul of souls and of worlds of Indian pantheism."[8] Rather, Chu Hsi's thinking was agnostic, a nontheistic rationalism pulling Chinese thought down to earth away from anthropomorphic concepts of heaven or Shang-ti. It was a monism, not with a creator or a mind but with a cosmic principle. The impact of the Buddhist void and the Taoist Tao was momentous: Chinese concepts of ultimate reality became depersonalized.

If this *li* resides within the nature of every man or actually constitutes his nature, how did Chu Hsi account for the actions of men that are patently evil? Chu Hsi followed Ch'eng I's hint that there is a *chi*, a celestial endowment, in every man which can check or inhibit the full manifestation of his essential nature, the *li*. Ch'eng I had said, "The mind in itself is originally good. As it expresses itself in thoughts and ideas, it is sometimes good and sometimes evil."[9] The *chi* or ethereal endowment is

7 Quoted by Rene Grousset, *The Rise and Splendour of the Chinese Empire,* The University of California Press, Berkeley, 1965, p. 218.

8 *Ibid.,* pp. 218, 219.

9 deBary, I, 473.

not a sinful nature inherited from one's parents but a predilection for good or evil given it by the caprice of nature. That is, man receives from nature not only the perfect *li* but also the *chi,* which alters the expression of this perfect nature, either releasing it for goodness or twisting it into perverted actions. Hence the man himself is not culpable. Chu Hsi explained:

> The nature of all men is good, and yet there are those who are good from their birth and those who are evil from their birth. This is because of the inequality of the ethereal endowment. Moreover, amid the infinite variety of phenomena in the revolutions of the universe it may be seen that if the sun and moon are clear and bright, and the climate temperate and seasonable, the man born at such a time and endowed with such an ether is possessed of a pure and bright, sincere and honest disposition, and will be a good man. But if the sun and moon are darkened and the temperature unseasonable, it is due to the untoward ether in the universe and it is not surprising if the man endowed with such an ether is a bad man. The object of self-culture is to transform this ethereal endowment, but the task is exceedingly difficult to accomplish.[10]

This is a philosophy of universal humanism, a humanism derived not from the concepts of a Creator who created man in his own image but from a universal principle spontaneously imparting itself to the nature of man.

These optimistic views of human nature have obviously taken root in Chinese intellectual soil, for ruling by private judgment not impersonal law needs no explanation in Communist China today. Also, Marxist hopes for a utopia on earth once a political system achieves its goal of placing the means of production into the hands of the proletariat are cherished as achievable goals. Wang Yang-Ming (A.D. 1472-1528) turned Chu Hsi's "investigation of things" away from an investigation of the Classics to intuitive

[10] Chu Hsi, *The Philosophy of Human Nature,* tr. J. Percy Bruce, Probsthain and Company, London, 1922, p. 86.

knowledge. He said, "In the heart of every man there lives a Confucius."[11] His theories advanced the humanistic ideas beginning with Mencius and developed by Chu Hsi to their ultimate; the essence of the world and the *li* could be discovered within the heart of man through meditation. Congruence of theory with practice became an achievable goal. Hence today the Communist emphasis upon the unity of theory and practice, ideas spun out of the mind of Mao becoming instantly canonized without critical reference to history, psychology, medicine, or even logic—this finds ready acceptance by Chinese minds schooled in Wang Yang-Ming's epistemology.

THE CHINESE IN SOCIETY

All inquiry and debate among Chinese scholars were meant to establish man's place in society, harmoniously carrying out his particular role in that society. Relationship—not a relationship of man to God but of man to society—is a basic goal of Chinese thought from Confucius to Mao Tse-tung. The ideal Chinese man was for centuries called the *chun-tzü*—the ethical individual, socially adjusted, eschewing extremes. The *chun-tzü* ruled not through hereditary rights nor legalistic structures but through moral suasion. His actions were to be governed by the laws of heaven, by the ways of the sages, by fundamental goodness (*jen*) or altruism working spontaneously. Thus the Confucian political ideal was benevolent paternalism, guiding the affairs of society through men whose natures have been most thoroughly divested of *chi*.

In the wake of the infamous Opium War of the mid-nineteenth century, there were vigorous attempts by the Chinese gentry to effect technological and social reform along traditional Confucian lines. The self-strengthening

[11] Grousset, p. 265.

movement of Tseng Kuo-fan, the T'ung-chih Restoration of 1862-1874, the Hundred Days fiasco of K'ang Yu-wei, found slogans in the Classics and a philosophy in Sung Neo-Confucianism. This philosophy taught that the natural harmony of the universe should be reflected in human society, that the harmony of Chinese society depended upon hierarchical organizations and the performance of proper roles from top to bottom. The *li* of the universe was also the definer of man's role in society and provided the canonical sanction for proper behavior in the Confucian scheme of things. And a Confucian society was necessarily an agrarian society where trade, industry, and economic development for personal gain and profit were seen as enemies. Thus the felt need was to strengthen the fiber of the Chinese character, for in the final analysis it was the "gentleman pursuing virtue and learning rather than power and profit who would save China."[12] Reformers, then, do not create, invent, or innovate; they simply "guide social life and help maintain its own natural course."[13] The last great Confucian thinker was Liao P'ing (1852-1932), who in an attempt to forestall the banishment of Confucius from modern Chinese thinking, heralded him as a prophet and reformer. He upheld Mencius as the forerunner of equal land distribution.

But the awesome display of Western technological superiority caused progressive Chinese thinkers to spurn this conservative idealism. With them the wave of the future was seen to be in Western pragmatism and rationalism. Hu Shih's (1891-1962) insistence that the language of the textbooks be the spoken language removed the Classics further from the rising generation. The debunkers did not believe that the ancient literati were sacrosanct but rather

12 deBary, II, 44.

13 Mary C. Wright, *The Last Stand of Chinese Conservatism: The T'ung-chih Restoration, 1862-1874,* Stanford University Press, Stanford, 1957, p. 3.

that they should be judged pragmatically in view of the modern needs of China. Hu Shih maintained that Mencius' equal-fields system (*chin-tien*) was merely social theory and never really existed in fact. Thus, sporadic attempts to give a Confucian stamp to the rising tide of socialism faltered. Later the Communists needed a whipping boy. Since Confucius had been identified with conservatism, warlordism, capitalism, Japanese imperialism, and despotism, he had to be attacked to insure a clean break with the past. Yet, if the Communists wanted to point to continuity, all the traits of the ideal man in Communist society could be found in the traditional past: the egalitarianism of Mo-tsu; the selection of a bureaucracy from the proletariat on the basis of merit; the persistent struggle to break up landed wealth and keep the land equally distributed among the peasant masses; the Taoist concept of the relativity of values, allowing for a break with the past and the setting up of Communist norms for good and evil; the universalist concept of Neo-Confucianism, allowing Western Marxist ideas to be adopted on Chinese soil, not as debts to the West but as timeless principles belonging to all. And the Old Legalism of Hsün-tzu could serve the police state well. So we see man in modern Chinese society donning the Communist ideological cloak but never actually doffing the erstwhile Confucian one. From Confucius to Mao Tse-tung the Chinese man stands in society as perfectible and potentially good but in practice evil, needing coercion until every vestige of evil (capitalism) is gone. Doak Barnett says:

> The question that may be most significant, however, is whether in the past there have been certain fundamental characteristics of Chinese society, which, when China's initial brief experiment with parliamentary and democratic government failed, predisposed the Chinese to accept modern totalitarianism. Certainly one can say that the dominant political tradition in China has been one of authoritarianism, centraliza-

tion and control. Did this provide a basis, after democracy had been discredited, for the establishment of modern communism?[14]

THE CHINESE LIFE GOAL

This humanism begins and ends with man. Chinese tradition from Confucius to Mao Tse-tung yielded no greater life goal than Ssu-ma Ch'ien records in his biography of Confucius, written in the second century before Christ: "The superior man hates the thought of his name not being mentioned after his death.... We must look to mankind for our own reward, the reward of a good or a bad name."[15] Immortality is achieved by continuing one's social achievements through the lives of one's posterity. The depersonalizing of heaven closed the Chinese in upon themselves—the hereafter became simply history immortalized.

CHINESE SOCIAL REFORM

Turning from phenomenology to history we must ask, Have these ideas about man produced modern social reform? That they had tremendous influence upon Chinese cultural progress until the modern period cannot be disputed. They achieved for China one of the greatest civilizations of the world. Marco Polo visited China during the magnificent Yuan dynasty of the Mongols (A.D. 1279-1368) and marvelled at her sophisticated culture—her silks, porcelains, paper money, printing techniques, ships, and military machines. In fact, until the seventeenth century more inventions flowed out of China than into it. She disdained all foreign visitors, either those journeying over-

14 A. Doak Barnett, *Communist China in Perspective,* Frederick A. Praeger, New York, 1962, p. 47.

15 Burton Watson, *Ssu-ma Ch'ien: Grand Historian of China,* Columbia University Press, New York, 1963, p. 157.

land from Central Asia or those from the West, plying the waters around Macao and Canton. Those outside the Chinese cultural ambit were one and all barbarians. Commissioner Lin on behalf of Peking reminded Queen Victoria in his famous letter of 1839 of some painful facts about life in Ch'ing China: "Articles coming from the outside to China can only be used for toys. We can take them or get along without them. Since they are not needed by China, what difficulty would there be if we closed the frontier and stopped the trade?"[16]

Prior to the modern period, which for our purposes begins with the Opium War of 1839-1842, Western learning had been introduced into China by Catholic missionaries. Jesuits like Matteo Ricci and Adam Schall von Bell arrived early in the seventeenth century. They brought with them medieval European culture and ideas, some as obsolete as Chinese ideas. Seven thousand volumes of Western learning accompanied them. By the end of the seventeenth century the Jesuits had translated some 380 works on science and mathematics—astronomy, Euclidean geometry, cartography, etc. However, the Western ideas they introduced were understood by only a small coterie of Chinese scholars. China looked incredulously at these strange creatures from the West, then assigned them the status of "barbarians"—fitting epithet for cultural inferiors outside the pale of the Middle Kingdom.

The West, however, could not be put off so easily. In the early nineteenth century, European powers clamored before China's gates, seeking trade privileges. The 1840 confrontation with the British over the rising opium traffic alarmed the Chinese populace. For this clash revealed that China's ancient defenses were simply not strong or mobile enough to ward off the foreign intruder. After a precarious peace was restored by the infamous unequal treaties with

[16] deBary, II, 7.

Western powers from 1842-58, Protestant missionaries came to the treaty ports and began teaching Biblical ideas to the common people. Some of these ideas captured the imagination of a band of seditious peasants called the Taipings.

The Taiping Rebellion of 1851-1864 mounted a challenge to the Chinese empire that shook the nation to its very foundations. What is pertinent to us, however, is that the Taipings attempted to reform Chinese society not in terms of traditional Chinese thinking, but according to Protestant Christianity. Yet even then, as we shall see, traditional Confucian ideas circumscribed the Chinese rebels, providing ideological control in the selection of Christian doctrines.

The Taiping Rebellion drew worldwide attention and sympathy, partly because it seemed to be inspired by doctrines found in the Protestant Bible. Here were simple Chinese peasants taking ideas from the Bible, living by them in their communes, spurred on to bring about a new social order in China. Except for one brief incident at the beginning of the founder's career, foreign missionaries had little contact with the movement. But they were jubilant when they heard of the radical outbursts of the rebels against Buddhist idolatry and their fanatical zeal in establishing Christian centers in China's hinterland. Sixteen thousand pounds were raised in England for printing one million Chinese New Testaments.

However, when the missionaries began to look closer, they were appalled. The rebels were resorting to violence. The Scriptures they applied were misinterpreted, distorted, taken out of context; these revolutionaries were submitting not to God but to their visible leader, Hung Hsiu-ch'üan, who claimed to be a younger brother of Jesus and the recipient of direct revelations from God. The rebellion was finally suppressed in 1864 at great loss of life and property to the Manchu regime. Thereafter, the missionary movement could not divest itself of a cloak of suspicion clinging to its endeavors, for the Rebellion did much to confirm deep-seated feelings among Chinese thinkers that after all Christianity was heterodox, a threat to their time-honored traditions. It will be our task to separate from traditional Chinese elements those distinctively Christian ideas which the rebels found useful in their new society. We must also understand why some Christian doctrines were rejected as incompatible with their Heavenly Kingdom.

The Rebellion grew "out of a situation compounded of dynastic decline, agrarian distress, overpopulation, foreign penetration, failure to provide adequate officialdom, and Chinese resentment against the misrule of alien Manchu overlords."[17] As in most dynastic declines, the incumbent government attempted to shore up the sagging regime with practices that if successful would be temporizing at best, and, if unsuccessful, exacerbate problems. For instance, to provide funds for its impoverished treasuries, the government resorted to a practice known as "contribution for appointment to public office," whereby the degrees requisite to a given position and usually acquired by competitive examination were sold to provide government funds.[18] This of course was a shortsighted measure. It secured funds but also caused dissatisfaction in those who were honestly seeking government office through the examination system. Hung Hsiu-ch'üan, leader of the Rebellion, was such a malcontent. He was born in 1814 in the district of Hua-hsien, about thirty miles from Canton. His father was a farmer. Thus Hung grew up in simple surroundings, devoid of foreign influence. He showed a flare for academics, so

[17] E. P. Boardman, *Christian Influence Upon the Ideology of the Taipings*, University of Wisconsin Press, Madison, 1962, p. 9.

[18] *Ibid.*, p. 10.

the family worked to keep him at the books. At the age of thirteen he qualified at the subprefectural level. At sixteen he tried and failed in the prefectural exams. Candidates who failed there were allowed to take the lower level circuit exams. He tried these tests in 1833, 1837, and 1843, failing all three times. Repeated failure at the only process that led to an official career did much towards making Hung a revolutionary. During the first sitting for the exams in 1833 or 1834, Hung heard a foreign evangelist preach and was given a set of nine tracts written by Liang A-fa (1789-1855), a convert of William Milne. He only glanced at these, then put them away. After failing the third time, Hung had a nervous breakdown. During his thirty-day convalescence he claimed to have visions, one of which took him to heaven, where he appeared before a venerable old man who represented himself as the Creator of mankind. The old man complained to Hung about two things: the widespread worship of demons and the fact that Confucius failed to expound clearly the true doctrine. During another such vision, Hung met a middle-aged man, whom he called his Elder Brother. The man instructed him on how to kill demons. For six years after his illness, Hung continued to teach in a village school. In 1843, his cousin borrowed the tracts and upon reading them suggested that Hung do likewise. The tracts confirmed Hung's convictions that the old man he had seen was God the Creator, and the middle-aged man, Jesus Christ. Hung himself was to be the second son of God, commissioned by God to redeem the world and bring China back to the worship of the true God. He learned the rite of baptism, whereupon he and his cousin Li Ching-fang baptized each other. A prominent feature of the movement that developed was its iconoclasm; Hung himself was expelled from his village for destroying Confucian tablets. As the number of followers grew, they called themselves *Pai Shang Ti Hui* (God-worshippers). In 1847 Hung heard that a foreigner in

Canton was preaching doctrines similar to his own and he travelled there to meet Issachar Roberts, a Southern Baptist missionary. Roberts listened to his story and accepted him as a seeker. After two months of instruction Hung offered himself for baptism, also suggesting that he be supported after baptism. "The advice to put forth such a request may well have been a trick on the part of fellow-countrymen in Roberts' establishment who were envious of Hung's ability and zeal and desirous of eliminating a competitor."[19] This so displeased Roberts that he postponed the baptism. Hung returned home, having no means of support. In 1849, because of the rise of banditry, Hung and his followers organized themselves for protection against such attacks. Their good organization attracted other harassed groups. Secret seditious societies joined them, for it appeared that their interests were not merely religious but also political and economic. Soon in an area called Thistle Mountain the rebels gained strength, employing the military titles found in *Chou-li* (*The Rites of Chou*), a Confucian Classic. A stern moral code was kept, infractions of which were punishable by death. The God-worshippers were required to dispose of their property, and proceeds were turned over to the Sacred Treasury. Money so collected was used to buy metal for smelting into weapons and bullets. Soldiers who risked death were told that all who died in battle would go directly to heaven. Orders or visions for the future were claimed to come through revelations from God or the Elder Brother Jesus. The record of these pronouncements was made the official book of the rebels, called the *Book of Heavenly Decrees and Imperial Edicts.* As the numbers grew, a primitive communal life developed; the people were given food, clothing, flags, and organized into military units. Strict separation of sexes was maintained. Members were

19 *Ibid.*, p. 44.

ordered to let their hair grow and cover it with a red cloth. They became known as the Long-Haired Rebels.

In their first clashes with government troops, the Taipings were signally victorious. One victory in 1851 was celebrated in a public ceremony of prayer and thanksgiving. On this occasion at Yung-an, Hung called himself the Heavenly King and his regime the *tai-p'ing t'ien-kuo* (Heavenly Kingdom of Great Peace). In March of 1853, the rebels captured Nanking, and one by one other cities along the Yangtse also fell. However, the rebel fortunes began to turn after some disastrous campaigns in the north, where the severe cold and the superior cavalry tactics of the northern defenders turned them back. Also responsible for the Taiping reverses were the campaigns of the loyalist Ever-Victorious Army, trained in artillery by the American soldier of fortune, Frederick T. Ward, and later led by Chinese Gordon. Finally, the scholar-official Tseng Kuo-fan mounted the government counterattack, laying siege to Nanking, and retaking it in July, 1864, thereby putting down the rebellion.

The failure of the Taipings was due largely to nonmilitary factors. They at first appealed to large segments of the Chinese population as a movement to redress the wrongs committed by the alien Manchu leaders. The Manchus, the Taipings charged, usurped Chinese property, forced the Chinese to wear the ignominious queue and non-Chinese dress, and always positioned Chinese troops in the vanguard while they remained rearward. They sold offices, turning the traditional examination system into a farce. But the Taipings failed to capture the support of the majority or effect a lasting reform in China because they were plagued with internal dissension and inconsistencies among the leaders, they did not carry out a thorough land reform, and they were poor administrators of captured cities. Efforts to staff the new government with truly qualified men were doomed to failure by faltering measures to create a workable examination system and prevent nepotism. But more decisive, since the Taipings threatened the status of traditional Chinese thought, loyal Chinese rallied to quell rebel Chinese in order to save the alien Manchus. For in the final analysis, their cultural heritage was more important than nationality.

However, Taiping revolutionary ideas on social reform were hailed by both Dr. Sun Yat Sen and the Communists. The Taipings envisaged the abolition of private ownership of land and property, followed by equal land distribution. Administrators had to be both military and civil leaders, giving themselves to spiritual and temporal affairs. Farmers were required to work at some industrial occupation between harvest seasons. A new calendar was adopted. With puritanical zeal they strictly maintained the equality of the sexes; enforced laws against the use of opium, tobacco, and alcohol; outlawed footbinding, slavery, prostitution, and gambling; enacted measures to support orphans and widows. Thomas Meadows visited the Heavenly Kingdom at Nanking in April, 1853, and was so impressed that he advised London to maintain strict neutrality during the upheaval:

> It would be sad to see Christian nations engaged in putting down the movement, as the insurgents possess an energy, and a tendency to improvement and general reform which the Imperialists never have exhibited, and never can be expected to display. Questionable though it be, the form of Christianity which the insurgents profess is far better than the stupid idolatry hitherto practised by the Chinese; and it is possible that European nations, if engaged on the opposite side, would be going to war with some people in some respects better than themselves. . . .[20]

[20] Immanuel Hsü, *The Rise of Modern China,* Oxford University Press, New York, 1970, p. 289.

The ideology of the Taipings, however, is the point we must discuss. It was a curious blend of Christian and Confucian ideas. They insisted on reverence for God, but their second commandment was filial piety. Jesus was the Son of God, but Hung a second Son, the new Son of Heaven, having received the Mandate of Heaven. They taught the brotherhood of men, but also rigidly held to a social hierarchy "in which the *li* or ancient principles of proper conduct were invoked to put everyone in his place by title, form of address, occupational class, and social relationships."[21] They offered sacrifice to God, not only animals but wine, tea, and rice. Elements of Taoist and Buddhist ritual crept into Taiping cultic celebrations—the use of drums, firecrackers, cakes, and fruit. They observed baptism and kept the Sabbath but used flags instead of the Cross. Only a small segment of Christ's life appears in the writings of the rebels. But Christ's resurrection was important, for it gave credence to their claim that Christ had appeared on earth again, this time to Hung in China. However, commands on forgiveness, humility, love for one another and one's enemies, the Golden Rule—these doctrines were passed over by the Taipings. If accepted, such doctrines would have made their violent, irresponsible actions reprehensible. The distinctively Christian ideas responsible for reform under the Taipings were respect for the dignity and equality of women, the honoring of marriage and monogamy (though Hung himself had eighty-eight concubines), a primitive communal type of life, and the importance of instruction for all by the ruling officers. At the same time, their communal use of land and their stress on hierarchy and military organization were variants of models found in the Classics, such as the *Chou-li* (*The Rites of Chou*).

21 John Fairbank, Edwin Reischauer, and Albert Craig, *East Asia: The Modern Transformation,* Houghton Mifflin Company, Boston, 1964, p. 161.

What has been the Taiping legacy to modern China? Dr. Sun Yat Sen, founder of the Republic of 1912, read about the rebellion as a boy and decided he would be a second Hung. Later, profiting by their errors, he added democracy and nationalism to Taiping socialism in forming his Three People's Principles. In effect, Sun carried out the social revolution they began. Communist scholars today hail the Taiping rebellion as the first Chinese peasant revolution of the modern era. Already in the Taiping ideology lay such fundamental Communist ideas as the ideal utopian state, the commune, egalitarianism, the abolition of private property, equal land distribution, and the notion that military power should be based on the peasants.

The immediate effect of Western imperialism and the Taiping insurgency on nineteenth-century China was to stimulate movements toward internal reform. Having narrowly averted dynastic catastrophe, the Ch'ing court found itself once more appealing to its traditional concepts. Celestial harmony, the order of nature reflected once more in the world of men—this would renovate Chinese society, strengthen it, and bring it abreast of the Western powers. Reform movements within the Confucian-structured social order commenced in 1862, continuing sporadically until the examination system was abolished in 1905 and the Republic founded in 1912. Some reforms were realistic, most were not; but all were meant to help Chinese society reflect the natural order of the universe.

The T'ung-chih Restoration from 1862-1874, for example, was a union-for-order and came as a last stand of Chinese conservatism,

> a conservatism aimed at the preservation of the Confucian, rationalistic gentry and nonfeudal strains of pre-Taiping and pre-Opium War Chinese society. . . . Chinese conservatism is part of a harmonious and rational natural order; willingness to subordinate private property to group interests; belief in man's innate goodness and his perfectibility through moral training;

> the honoring of custom not as a brake on reason but as the embodiment of reason; and the persistent ideal of the universal state.[22]

Such prominent scholar-officials as Feng Kuei-fen (1809-1874), Tseng Kuo-fan (1811-1872), and Li Hung-chang (1823-1901) rallied to save China from imminent danger. Their basic ideas were developed from Sung Neo-Confucianism, which said that the organizing principle of the universe, the *li,* was to govern human society and define proper roles, creating a hierarchy "in which every human being understands his duties and his privileges and accepts them as a part of a rational and universal natural order."[23] Quoting Mencius' words, "If you can rule your own country, who dares insult you?"[24] Tseng began reform along all lines—diplomatic, fiscal, educational, and military. The Office of Foreign Affairs (*Tsungli-yamen*) was established in 1861. The Maritime Customs Service, staffed by English personnel with Irishman Robert Hart as the guiding light, became a reliable source of revenue for the government, characterized by honesty and efficiency. Machine shops, arsenals, and shipyards were built in Anking, Soochow, Nanking, and Shanghai. The examination system was reinstated with testing periods fixed, local academies set up, libraries built, classical books reprinted. Examination questions became more pragmatically oriented to the present; sale of degrees declined. However, the emphasis of the T'ung-chih movement was more on men than on institutions, a strengthening of Chinese character according to the prescription of the *li*. And, as ever, the prescription called for virtue and learning, not the development of theories leading to economic, industrial, and military power.

22 Wright, p. 1.
23 *Ibid.,* p. 3.
24 Fairbank, p. 315.

Though much was accomplished, the T'ung-chih Restoration was wholly inadequate. For the ideal society under the *li* was one of "static harmony, not of dynamic growth."[25] The Restoration was committed to two fundamental beliefs of traditional China, namely that agriculture was the economic ground for China's livelihood and that a group of ruling officials chosen for their scholarly achievement formed the basis of good government.

And, as in India, the ontocratic pattern of society stifled reform. Since in such a view the past dominates the present, the would-be reformer is a mere restorer who attempts to lock a fragmented society again into a universal order of regularity, hierarchy, harmony, decorum, and role playing. Confucian bureaucrats who received a mandate for change from the practical realities of nineteenth-century China accepted it as a mandate to update, paradoxically, a timeless order. The very ones who could have innovated and stepped into the future began marking time in the halls of the past. Self-strengthening continued after 1874, the lead being taken by provincial leaders such as Li Hung-chang (1823-1901) and Chang Chih-tung (1837-1909). In 1885 Chang on his own initiative began to establish modern institutions at Canton and Hanyang: iron foundries and technical schools for teaching telegraphy, mining, and industrial arts. Though known for his anti-foreignism, Chang nevertheless sought advice from the Welsh missionary, Dr. Timothy Richard (1845-1919). Richard, a Christian progressive who had already struggled against famine in Shansi, believed that the Kingdom of God was to "be established not only in the hearts of men, but also in all institutions on earth, [that] those who did their best to improve this world were best fitted for eternal bliss hereafter."[26] His writings on social reform, as we shall see,

25 *Ibid.*, p. 328.
26 *Ibid.*, p. 364.

influenced the thinking of many progressive scholar-officials.

But all was not clear sailing. Though there were some notable exceptions, such as Chang Chien (1853-1926), the scholar-industrialist, most of the gentry class, tied by traditional views, gave little thought to government encouragement of industry. If such industry did develop, theirs was to observe, umpire, and even personally invest. But government revenue would come from taxation of land and farm produce. Their security lay in the examination system, and they would not tamper with it. Tseng, for example, though an enthusiastic advocate of self-strengthening, was ignorant of economic processes. The idea of economic competition as an outlet for nationalism was a foreign idea. The concept of progress, implying continual change, self-criticism, innovation, and industrial research, was not considered. The conflict of traditional ideas with the demands of modern development doomed railway enterprises before the first spikes were driven. A small line opened by Jardine, Matheson and Company between Shanghai and Wusung in 1876 was purchased by the Nanking governor, who then destroyed it. Reasons? The railroad would have offered undue competition to water transport and the line cut across Chinese property, upsetting geomancy and grave mounds.

Such conservatism throttled movements toward modernization. China moved inevitably toward a stinging defeat of her land and naval forces in the Sino-Japanese War of 1894-1895. Leaders in Peking were shocked by this catastrophe. Memorials to the throne began pouring in from alarmed patriots. One such patriot was K'ang Yu-wei (1858-1927), a holder of the *chüjen* degree. On behalf of more than 1200 candidates taking the examinations for the *chin-shih* degree in Peking, he vigorously protested the provisions of the Shimonoseki Treaty with Japan. This action precipitated the last great self-strengthening movement of the century, beginning in 1895 and climaxing in the Hundred Days Reform fiasco of the summer of 1898. K'ang had previously visited the foreign settlements of Hongkong and Shanghai. There he was very much impressed with the well-governed colonies of the Europeans, and he concluded that "European society must have a solid foundation of moral principles, as well as of political and natural sciences."[27] Thereupon K'ang purchased and read translations of Western books on industry, military science and medicine, as well as the Bible.

Other scholars, such as Liang Ch'i-ch'ao (1873-1929), joined K'ang in forming the Society for the Study of Self-strengthening in 1895. Liang had previously served as Chinese secretary to Timothy Richard and now from that experience edited a daily periodical for the society. The periodical reprinted many articles dealing with reform that had been written by Young J. Allen (1836-1907), a missionary from Georgia. Liang and K'ang made a sharp dichotomy between Western technology and Chinese ethics. Heretofore most scholars had adopted the comforting line that Western technology was really what China had known all along but hadn't developed. Now they took the Japanese approach: Eastern ethics, Western science. Their slogan was "Chinese learning for essential principles, Western learning for the practical applications."[28] The Sung formula, *T'i-yung* (substance-function), used to distinguish inner ideas from their outward application, was re-interpreted "Eastern spirit, Western matter." Others tried to trace the origins of Western science to Chinese alchemy, asserting, for example, that the Chinese view of the five elements was the precursor of modern chemistry. Sanc-

[27] Victor Purcell, *The Boxer Uprising*, Cambridge University Press, Cambridge, 1963, pp. 102-103.

[28] Fairbank, p. 386.

tions for change had to be found in the traditional past. But the dynamics of change, the idea of progress emerging spontaneously from the human brain—these were missing ingredients in their ideas for reform. K'ang did, however, advance beyond Sung learning. He put forth the Modern Text idea that as Confucius had been a reformer in the name of the past, so modern China should reform in the name of Confucius. He advocated the theory of Three Ages—(1) disorder, (2) rising peace, and (3) great tranquility. With his recommended reforms China could now enter an age of rising peace. "In his hands the great tradition could become a modern revolution."[29]

But those scholar-officials charged with carrying out reform dragged their feet, knowing they had no real mandate until the empress-dowager expressed approval. Then Germany seized Kiaochow in Shangtung; other nations pressed for more concessions. K'ang's hour had come. At his first audience with Emperor Kuang-hsü on June 16, 1898, he urged immediate adoption of sweeping reforms with the words, "China will soon perish. All that is caused by the conservatives. If your majesty wishes to rely on them for reform, it will be like climbing a tree to seek for fish."[30] The emperor agreed. K'ang thereupon issued over forty edicts during the famous One Hundred Days. He ordered modern schools set up, the examination system refurbished, new approaches to be taken in the study of agriculture, medicine, mining, commerce, and in training abroad. The army, navy, police, and postal departments would be modernized. But such radical reforms would, of course, jeopardize the whole Confucian social order, and with it all those who had a vested interest in this order. The twenty-seven-year-old emperor began experiencing a conservative backlash, and was eventually seized and

29 *Ibid.*, p. 389.
30 *Ibid.*, p. 392.

forced into a seclusion by the empress dowager. K'ang and Liang fled to Japan; other reformers were executed. The Confucian order had been shaken, but remained very much intact.

In retrospect we must ask, since K'ang advocated reform beyond the existing Confucian scheme of things, where did his revolutionary ideas come from—ideas which if accepted might have averted the violence that erupted over a decade later? Did the old world view itself somehow encourage China to lift herself up, critically reflect over her achievements and deficiencies, and then work for a new China? Or did the motivations for such reflection and vision come from another quarter? Timothy Richard was able to interview the emperor's tutor in 1895. Later the emperor and his tutor read daily from Richard's translation of Mackenzie's *The Nineteenth Century.* In the introduction, Richard had asked,

> What is the cause of the foreign wars, indemnities, and repeated humiliations suffered by China during the last 60 years? . . . God has been breaking down the barriers between all nations by railways, steamers and telegraphs, in order that we should all live in peace and happiness as brethren of one family; but the Manchus, by continual obstruction, were determined from the first to prevent this intercourse. . . . If this attitude were changed, China might still become one of the greatest nations on earth.[31]

K'ang too had been influenced by Richard and Allen. He said in a private interview, "I owe my conversion [to reform] chiefly to the writings of two missionaries, the Reverend Timothy Richard and the Reverend Doctor Young J. Allen."[32]

At the turn of the century another indefatigable challenger to the old system arose in the person of Sun Yat

31 Purcell, p. 116.

32 Cyrus H. Peake, *Nationalism and Education in Modern China,* New York, 1932, p. 15.

Sen (1866-1925). Sun went to Honolulu at the age of thirteen and was enrolled in an Anglican school. He sang in a church choir and accepted Christianity. His childhood impressions of life in China were impressions of poverty, official corruption, banditry, ignorance, and superstition. In contrast, at the Anglican school he found "security, justice, and fairmindedness; comfortable, middle class English standards; education which was to a child anyway more apparently modern than the Three Character Classic."[33] When Sun returned to China, conditions in his village were worse than when he left it. He concluded that the old views could serve China no more and became a revolutionary. Lincoln's slogan "government of the people, by the people, for the people" fascinated him. After some abortive attempts to overthrow the Manchus, Sun was forced to flee to Japan. From Japan he travelled around the world seeking aid for his cause from overseas Chinese as well as from Western financiers. The final coup de grace was administered the Manchu dynasty by the Wuchang uprising of soldiers on October 10, 1911. Sun was in Denver, Colorado, at the time but hastened home to be elected the provisional president of the first constitutional Chinese Republic January 1, 1912. His Three Principles of nationalism, democracy, and socialism (*san min chu i*) became pillars of reform. Today, both the Nationalist Party (KMT) in Taiwan and the Chinese Communist Party (CCP) in Peking hail Sun as a great leader of their movements. Official Communist history describes Sun as an "incorruptible patriot," "the boldest and most radical," while Chiang Kai-shek rallies all anti-Mao forces under the banner of Sun's Three Principles.

Communist ideas began to affect Sun's thinking in the early '20's. Frustrated by the indifference of the Western

[33] Bernard Martin, *Sun Yat Sen's Vision for China,* The China Society, London, 1966, p. 7.

powers during his efforts to overthrow the Manchus, Sun welcomed Russian assistance. In 1923, Michael Borodin visited KMT leaders as the official agent of the Comintern and helped draft a new constitution. The story of the rise of Communism in China is beyond this study, but it will be instructive to ask how Chinese intellectuals during the '20's were able to make the transition from Confucianism to Communism. After observing the spectacle of Western powers butchering one another in World War I, many Chinese thinkers concluded that Western and Chinese ideals were actually opposed. These intellectuals turned nationalistic and found themselves caught in the dilemma of trying to "disparage the Chinese past and to prize it, to admire the West and to grudge the admiration."[34] Communism could serve as an ideology by which to break with China's past and march into the future, admitting no failure, suffering no debtor's complex.

> Intellectuals who were alienated from their own tradition could never rest easy with a westernization which seemed to enjoin on China a spirit of humility; for them, the existence in the West of revolutionary ideas, critical of the very civilization which had impinged on China, offered one way out. No longer had China either to cling to a moribund system or to defer respectfully to a West of challenging prestige.[35]

MISSIONARIES AND SOCIAL REFORM

By his very presence in China the missionary was a bearer of an alien culture. The missionary came to do something in China; he was a constant agent of change. The vast hinterland of China with its millions having no fanatical faith to thwart missionary efforts appeared a promising field. "The Chinese world resembled the European classical world in that the ruling class were philo-

[34] J. R. Levenson, *Liang and the Mind of Modern China,* p.3.
[35] *Ibid.,* pp. 5, 6.

sophic pagans, more interested in ethical doctrine than in religious beliefs, and the mass of the people polytheists who had no theological prejudices, but merely worshipped their gods with traditional rites."[36] But the ancient Chinese perspectives actually posed more of a problem than the missionaries anticipated. First, the concept of a universal order on earth had made the Chinese tolerant of *any* religion as long as it posed no threat to that order. Thus, they found it difficult to grant to the Christian faith the uniqueness it claimed. Second, the dominance of religious humanism made transcendentalism seem superstitious. Belief in God or gods was illiterate and uncivilized. "The educated believe in nothing, the uneducated believe in everything" was a common saying. Third, since Shang ti had become depersonalized through Neo-Confucianism to the point where an impersonal *li* now governed the universe, talk about a personal Creator-God sounded anachronistic.

In the seventeenth century, the Jesuits had attempted to make peace with Chinese tradition by clarifying Confucius' ideas in the context of general revelation. They worked from the top down, seeking to make the emperor a Chinese Constantine. Not a sharp break with the past but a slow transformation within the traditional Chinese structure was the goal of Catholic missions. J. Hudson Taylor (1832-1905) with his cry, "A million a month in China dying without God" sent hundreds of missionaries into distant provinces. Among those millions were the elect of God. These individuals would be found by scattering the seed of the Gospel wide and far. Social efforts—clinics, hospitals, schools—were undertaken to attract as large a following as possible, so that from among thousands the elect might be found.

[36] C. P. Fitzgerald, *Birth of Communist China*, Penguin Books, Baltimore, 1964, p. 121.

Though their main energies were devoted to evangelism, missionaries also played an important role in social reform. Their literary efforts were devoted initially to Bible translation and the preparation of religious tracts. But eventually some gifted linguists began translating secular works as well. W. A. P. Martin translated Wheaton's *Elements of International Law.* He was also instrumental in developing a school of Western languages and sciences called the T'ung-wen Kuan, which sent forth trained Chinese into the diplomatic corps. Alexander Wylie contributed many translations in the field of mathematics, completing Books 7-15 of Euclid's *Elements* begun by Ricci in the seventeenth century. In 1877, a Text Book Series Committee was appointed by the missionaries and was responsible for the production of a large number of books for the growing Christian schools.

As the Self-strengthening Movement regained momentum, missionaries moved in concert with it, directing their literary talents toward China's practical needs. Immanuel Hsü says,

> Of the 795 titles translated by Protestant missionaries between 1810 and 1867, 86 per cent were in religion, and only 6 per cent in the humanities and sciences. During the 1861-1895 Self-strengthening Movement, translations extended into diplomacy, military arts, science and technology. Of 567 works translated between 1850 and 1899, 40 per cent were in applied sciences, 30 per cent in natural sciences, 10 per cent in history and geography, 8 per cent in social sciences, and about 3.5 per cent in religion, philosophy, literature, and the fine arts.[37]

Missionary educational efforts were nothing less than spectacular. As Protestant educational institutions grew in number, Chinese students found themselves in a dilemma: either enter government service by graduating from state-

37 Hsü, p. 504.

sponsored schools hidebound in classical studies or enter private enterprise (without status) by graduating from progressive mission-sponsored schools. In 1876 there were 4,909 pupils in 209 mission schools. In 1906, there were 57,683 pupils; by 1911 there were 56,000 pupils in mission primary schools and 45,000 pupils in higher schools. Yung Wing (1828-1912), for example, learned English from the age of seven in missionary schools and was sent by missionaries to the United States. He became a Christian and graduated from Yale in 1854. Yung's vision of sending an educational mission of Chinese boys to America was finally approved by the government in 1872. One hundred twenty boys went, dressed in Chinese garb. They lived in private homes and quickly became Americanized. However, they were viewed with suspicion upon their return to China. Only twelve of their number were finally admitted into officialdom; the rest had to content themselves with positions requiring the knowledge of Western technology in private industry.

But overall, China benefited directly and indirectly by these missionary efforts for education. When the Republic was finally established in 1912, China had leaders familiar with Western ways and democratic thinking, men who had been trained in mission schools. Three of the five delegates to the Paris Peace Conference (1919) were prominent Christians—C. T. Wang of the YMCA, Wang Ch'ung-hui, chief judge of the Supreme Court, and W. S. Yen, one-time premier. Indirectly, by their demonstrated willingness to teach anyone regardless of status, missionaries showed a concern for the individual. Democracy is born from concepts of the individual standing as a foundational unit in society. But such ideas do not occur in a hierarchal culture such as characterized traditional China.

Missionaries also fought tirelessly against social evils—opium smoking, infanticide, polygamy, fortune-telling, prostitution. They attacked these first by proclaiming deliverance through Christ, and secondly by offering practical help to those earnestly seeking it. Kenneth S. Latourette sums up the moral persuasiveness of the Christian message:

> Now a man wished to be free from the opium habit, and found release through his new faith; often he hoped for the aid of the missionary in a lawsuit; occasionally someone who had been vainly seeking inward peace through the religious agencies known to him discovered it in the Christian Gospel; sometimes the attraction was the moral emphasis of Christianity and the changed lives of those already Christians, and sometimes what the applicant had seen and heard while in a hospital. Occasionally the catechumen was drawn by intellectual belief in the superiority of Christianity, sometimes by the promise of eternal life, and often by a conviction of the futility of idolatry as an aid in obtaining the goods of this life and by confidence that these could be secured through the Christians' God.[38]

The Nanking Decade from 1928 to 1938 was a high-water mark of Christian social reform activity. Protestant missionaries numbered 8,300 by 1935, over half of whom were American. They had unparalleled opportunities to work despite the depression and mounting criticism of missionary strategy at home. Encouragement came from an unexpected quarter. After Chiang Kai-shek's marriage to the American-educated Methodist Soong Mei-ling, he professed conversion to Christianity. His tacit approval of missionary endeavors, in contrast to the hostility of Communism and the spectre of Japanese imperialism, led to renewed bursts of energy among Protestants toward social reform. Their efforts were first directed toward the rural crisis. Spiraling population increases without the corresponding development of new agricultural land made the problem acute. No effective land reform measures had been undertaken by the Manchus. And Sun's plan for the

[38] K. S. Latourette, *A History of Christian Missions in China, 1924-1949,* Ch'eng-Wen Publishing Company, Taipei, pp. 480-481.

equalization of land ownership according to Georgian principles had been thwarted by the fragmenting of centralized government into warlordism. The National Christian Council in China, embracing the social implications of the Gospel, encouraged the church to strive against poverty as well as paganism. At the International Missionary Council in Jerusalem in 1928, Kenyon Butterfield, an agricultural expert, gave a report on the Christian role in agricultural communities and urged a "rural community parish." He then came to China in November of 1930 and recommended a "community parish, with a self-supporting rural church, indigenous in its methods, led by a specially trained pastor, who was to be both 'a preacher and a community leader and builder'."[39] Chang Fu-liang, an educator and agriculturalist trained at Yale and the University of Georgia, sparked the rural rehabilitation program in Kiangsi in 1934. James Yen, a Yale graduate serving with the YMCA, developed a simple 1,000-character approach for teaching illiterate peasants. He believed that the key to rural reform was mass education. Church authorities, at first indifferent, finally sent delegates to his Tinghsien Literacy Institute in April, 1930. This was a turning point for both social reform and evangelism in rural China; now foreign and national evangelists could go to the countryside and assist in the literacy program while propagating the faith.

Madame Chiang visited Methodist missionary William Johnson in 1933 with two requests. She asked Johnson to find a missionary couple to take charge of an orphanage in Nanking and secondly to study the problem of rural reconstruction in Kiangsi on a large scale under mission auspices. Kiangsi had been delivered from Communist control, but the plight of the villagers in the wake of hostilities was acute. Johnson met with church leaders of the NCC and

39 James Thomson, *While China Faced West: American Reformers in Nationalist China, 1928-1937*, p. 53.

also Rockefeller representatives. Shortly thereafter, an unprecedented invitation to the Christian church from the Chinese government came to the NCC. There was some hesitancy to accept the proposal. Wouldn't the Christian church become too closely identified with a government party (the KMT)? Wouldn't the church be seen espousing a particular economic theory? But despite these misgivings the project soon got underway under the leadership of the Christian Rural Service Union in Kiangsi. Its main program was education. Travelling seminars encouraged village organization, agricultural extension, public health, village industries, and religious training. Half of the $100,000 budget was supplied by the Chiangs and half by the NCC. The project finally developed under the direction of George Shepherd of the Congregational Church. Earlier Shepherd had fled Kiangsi, harassed by the Communists. When he finally returned to Kiangsi, he realized more than ever before the urgent need to help China's oppressed and underprivileged peasantry. He advocated Butterfield's "rural community parish" idea. He deplored the methods of the Communists but marvelled at their tenacity and could not fault their aims. He wrote in September, 1932: "Communism as a solution to the social problems of China is still commanding the attention and serious study of many students. Does Christianity offer any such crusade against the entrenched evils of society? This is a question that many are asking."[40] Observing James Yen's Rural Reconstruction Institute at Tinghsien, Shepherd wrote enthusiastically: "Jimmy Yen accomplishes all of the Red Program and more, in a way that is Christian and acceptable to all who still believe that Christ's principle of love and sacrifice is more powerful than violence and the sword."[41]

40 *Ibid.*, p. 79.
41 *Ibid.*, p. 81.

In the fall of 1933, Shepherd met Chiang Kai-shek for the first time. Chiang, knowing of Shepherd's first-hand knowledge of the Communist activities in Kiangsi, asked him many questions. Soon after Chiang suggested that Christian leaders follow in the wake of his KMT armies to undertake rural reconstruction. "We must organize the local Christians as soon as the armies enter a district," he said. "The Christian farmers and workers will be our right hand men in establishing law and order."[42] Shepherd had first come to China as an evangelistic missionary. But coming to grips with the hard realities of China–famine, devastation, poverty, illiteracy, ignorance–caused him to reorient his thinking about the Christian approach to underprivileged peoples. He discovered within Christianity a dynamic for social change. In a letter to his missionary colleague Fairfield in 1933, he said:

> We can help the world's toilers as we toil with them and bend together on the dusty road. This after all, in the spirit of our Master, may be our most lasting contribution. Others may reorganize villages and rural communities, teach self-defense, train the young, teach morality and religion or completely ignore them, improve agriculture and village industries, impart the principles of healthful living, organize cooperatives and self-governing units, solve the agrarian problem, etc., and we may do some or all of these, but only as we manifest the spirit of Him who went about doing good from early morn till late at night regardless of His own rights or comfort, and eventually gave up life itself in the interests of the people, shall we make this a truly Christian project and an answer to those who advocate violence as the only road to social reorganization.[43]

Shepherd's rural reconstruction ideas seemed the only viable solution to a Chinese hinterland seething with unrest. He believed that the best answer to a revolution imposed by force was a positive one carried out through

42 *Ibid.*, p. 87.
43 *Ibid.*, pp. 48, 88-89.

hard work, patience, and sacrifice. For Kiangsi he recruited volunteer laborers willing to work for subsistence. As the work gathered momentum, it became apparent to all that it was a movement spearheaded by Christianity. Shepherd became the Christian counterpart to the Soviet's Borodin.

In February of 1935, Chiang Kai-shek launched his New Life Movement to modernize China, develop rural communities, and raise China to a par with other nations. The success of the Christian Rural Reconstruction in Kiangsi encouraged Chiang to make a nationwide experiment. For this he sought first a new integrating and motivating force for uniting the people. He said, "The great need of society in China is an integrating force. In England and America this force is furnished by churches and kindred social organizations, and in Italy and Russia by the dominant party. . . . Our own national party has in many places lost public respect and cannot function as the needed force."[44] Chiang in an unprecedented move turned to the Chinese church to provide the leadership and cohesion for the movement. He decreed that "officials, teachers, students, military and police, should cooperate with the Y.M.C.A., for that is the clearing house of service for the churches in our large cities. Where there is no Y.M.C.A., a plan of cooperation with the churches directly should be worked out. . . . Western church leaders in our midst ought also to be utilized. Their attitude toward life is sane and sensible."[45] On his return from furlough in the autumn of 1935, Shepherd was asked by Chiang in Nanking to be a director of the New Life Movement. He had some misgivings about the relation of church and state, and how far the NCC should be identified with a political party, but he accepted the post. The following month of March, he lived with the Chiangs. Worship services were held in their

44 *Ibid.*, p. 165.
45 *Ibid.*

home. Shepherd's doubts were dissolving. "As one by one these leaders of the nation revealed their spiritual hunger, sang joyously the grand old hymns of the Christian Church, and united in prayer, I felt glad I had not turned them down."[46]

This was an auspicious beginning. However, to the regret of Christian missions and later the entire free world, the movement faltered. Incessant war with the Communists and Japan dissipated efforts towards rural reconstruction. Political corruption plagued the movement. During Shepherd's furlough in America in 1940, James Endicott assumed his position in the New Life Movement. The endeavor, bereft of Shepherd's dynamic leadership, began to sputter. In retrospect, Communist writers who were once in the movement now view the Christian Rural Reconstruction as American cultural aggression, a reaction against Communism. They denounce Shepherd as a secret agent and label the doctrine of brotherly love as a cloak for nefarious imperialism. One such writer, Y. T. Yu, says, "I began to comprehend the error of reformism and embarked upon the path of revolution."[47]

In conclusion let us summarize the relation of Confucianism, Nationalism, Christianity, and Communism to social reform. Confucianism is the embodiment of an idea—the idea that a universal heavenly order reflected in human relationships is the best way to achieve a stable society. After the demise of the Manchu dynasty in 1911, impersonal ideas of democracy could not fill the vacuum created by the loss of a universal empire. Thus Nationalism served as a cohesive ideal in a fragmented China during the short-lived years of the Republic. Nationalism was Sun Yat Sen's answer to alien Manchu rule and humiliating Western encroachments. It was Chiang's answer to the blandish-

46 *Ibid.*, p. 177.
47 *Ibid.*, p. 244.

ments of Japanese imperialism and the divisiveness of Communism. Yet, although Chiang used the services of missionary reformers during the Nanking Decade, he actually laid out the ideology of the New Life Movement along traditional Confucian lines. The new life was merely the old life prescribed by Confucianism—a social order in which everyone fulfills his proper role from top to bottom. Christianity came to China concerned with society, but more with the individual in that society. Its efforts toward social reform were by-products of its concern for the spiritual well-being of the individual. Then Communism came, appealing to many Chinese scholars as a more effective and faster modus operandi for reforming Chinese society. Social reform through free acts was painfully slow and often as not ended in social anarchy. Communism mounted the attack against both traditional Confucianism and Christianity. But it structured a new society in which the individual is again of secondary importance. This New Republic is not handicapped by popular sovereignty. Of course, congresses, parties, and elections are all there. "But this is organized participation, under the supervision of the vanguard party. Elections are ceremonies of support."[48] In one sense we can say that the old idea has survived the attack. The Confucian plan for a structured society based upon a hierarchal order has given way to the Communist plan for a society based upon class struggle to right the inequities created by the capitalistic accumulation of land and industry. Communism's final goal then, like that of Confucianism, is a harmonious society, not a society which tolerates differences and protects minority rights.

C. P. Fitzgerald summarizes as follows the relation of Confucianism, Christianity, and Communism in the struggle to modernize China:

[48] Robert Scalapino, *The Communist Revolution in Asia,* Prentice-Hall, Englewood Cliffs, New Jersey, 1965, p. 4.

> Yet it must be recognized that Christianity and the missions accomplished many things in China, though not the thing they most desired to do. They broke into the closed world of Confucian learning, and sowed there the seeds of scientific knowledge, of Western political thought, and of Western economic theory. They started the first hospitals in China, and the whole medical profession owes its origin to their teaching. . . . The Christian missions, staffed by men of different sects and various nationalities, showed that it was possible to have a world-wide faith, a system of values which was applicable in many countries. . . . It may be said that Christianity stormed first into the breach in the Confucian citadel; it was repelled and overcome; and on its back the ultimate victor, Communism, mounted to the assault.[49]

49 Fitzgerald, p. 135.

3

Japan

At least five world views have played a major role in the history of Japanese thought—Shintoism, Buddhism, Confucianism, Western humanism and existentialism. But above all these systems of thought there has stood one dominating, correlating cultural theme: Man is one with the cosmos. The congruence of Japanese festivals with the equinoxes and the New Year is no historical accident. For the Japanese have from ancient times wished to participate in nature's rejuvenating cycle each year. New Year's Day begins with self-purification and being reborn, as it were, in the cosmogonic cycle. Man is in the cosmos, participating in the cosmogony, intimately related to nature, seeking fulfillment here and now. That is, the cosmos itself has become the Japanese ground of being. Robert Bellah in *Tokugawa Religion* says: "Nature [to the Japanese] is both a . . . nurturing force toward whom man should express gratitude and a manifestation of the ground of being. Man may attain insight into the essence of reality and union with it through the apprehension of some natural form. Nature is not alien to the divine or to man but is united with both."[1]

[1] Robert Bellah, *Tokugawa Religion*, Free Press, Glencoe, Illinois, 1957, p. 62.

Thus "how" questions are more relevant to the Japanese than "what" questions. "How do I integrate my life with nature and man?" "How do I orient myself in the cosmos?" These are live issues. Philosophical questioning about the nature of man is an academic luxury few can afford. First one must fix his life goal. Then, if he must, he can select and adapt fragments of religious theories compatible to this goal. The Japanese man himself stands above any system of thought, be it Shinto, Confucian, Buddhist, humanist, existential, or Christian. But let us examine briefly what fragments of religious thought he has adopted for his journey through life.

THE JAPANESE MAN

Shinto has emphasized the union of man with the divine aspects of the cosmos. Man is in the state of godhead, not a transcendent godhead but a godhead within the divine, pure, aesthetic aspects of nature herself. This concept fuses the Japanese race together. All have descended from the mythological divinity Izanami, then later from Emperor Jimmu (660 B.C., supposedly), and the succeeding imperial line. The familial bond of the Japanese people with their ancestral gods (*kami*) gives them a peculiar cultural unity. It sets them off as a distinct race, linked to nature and to each other through the medium of the ubiquitous *kami*. This word *kami* eludes definition, but Norinaga Motoori gives the general sense: "It is hardly necessary to say that it [the *kami*] includes human beings. It also includes such objects as birds, beasts, trees, plants, seas, mountains, and so forth. In ancient usage, anything whatsoever which was outside the ordinary, which possessed superior power, or which was awe-inspiring, was called *kami*."[2] How do the mysterious *kami* create this Japanese

[2] Quoted in *Sources of the Japanese Tradition,* ed. William deBary, Columbia University Press, New York, 1964, I, 21.

solidarity? The religion organized around belief in the *kami* is called *Shinto,* a word coined by the Chinese and meaning "the Way of the Kami." Early Shinto revealed a cosmic orientation. People and acts had value or became real because they participated in a reality that transcended them—the *kami.* When people or things receive this exterior force, they become distinct from their milieu and acquire special significance. The effect of this concept upon the Japanese self-image was momentous. "What is involved," comments Mircea Eliade, "is creating man and creating him on a supra-human plane, a man-god, such as the imagination of historical man has never dreamed it possible to create."[3] This man-god is a member of the Yamato race, not by virtue of birth or language but by participation in the *kami.* And the Yamato race can be seized with a sense of national mission; her young men went out resolutely to bring all of Asia under the Japanese "roof" (*hakko ichiu*) in the Pacific War. For to serve the emperor is a moral act. Righteousness is not a religiously oriented concept but one of social duty. This was the tenor of the Imperial Rescripts, the Imperial messages to soldiers and sailors, and the national polity (*kokutai*). For example, the *Fundamentals of Our National Polity of 1937* sharply contrasts Western individualism as expressed in socialism, communism or democracy with the unity of the Japanese people, joined to the emperor and to the homeland by the divine *kami.*

Of course, the Japanese themselves seriously questioned the whole Yamato race concept after World War II, so that the term "spirit of Yamato" (*Yamato-damashi*) is used pejoratively in modern Japan. Yet, the same sense of the unity of the Japanese race is dominant in Japanese thinking today. It manifests itself when a foreigner tries to

[3] Mircea Eliade, *Cosmos and History,* Harper and Row, New York, 1959, p. 149.

identify with the Japanese people. No matter if he speaks impeccable Japanese, attends Japanese schools, lives in a Japanese home, entertains only Japanese guests, he is still considered a *gaijin* (translated "foreigner" but literally meaning "outsider"). This is not to imply that Japanese are inhospitable to foreigners or xenophobic. Kawasaki Ichiro says, "True, the average Japanese makes great efforts to make friends with a gaijin (foreigner of Caucasian extraction), but somehow or other he feels everything related to a foreigner is something quite alien to him, and often tries to retreat into his own mental and spiritual domain."[4] But more important, this solidarity concept tends to lose Japanese individuality within the peer group. Nakamura Hajime asserts:

> . . . The Japanese are always sensitive to efforts to establish compact relations among the individuals within a small closed community. This endeavor for mutual relationship serves to create a sense of unity and sympathy among the Japanese. But at the same time, it sometimes makes them accept blindly the principle of authority at the expense of individuality.[5]

What influence did Buddhism have upon Japanese concepts of man? Buddhist culture came in repeated waves to Japan from China during the Nara-Heian periods (A.D. 710-1159), bringing with it impressive literature, calligraphy, art, ritual, architecture, and philosophy. Theoretical Buddhism in India taught that the universe is ephemeral, full of sorrow, and soulless. The universe has no contradictory principles: opposites are apparent, not real. All contradictions are resolved in the great void (*ku*). It follows then that personality, individuality, and selfhood are illusory concepts. Man does not have an individual soul. He shares in the one, all-embracing Buddha-heart (*busshin*).

[4] Kawasaki Ichiro, *Japan Unmasked,* Charles E. Tuttle Company, Tokyo, 1969, p. 158.

[5] Nakamura, p. 466.

To reach ultimate reality man must free himself from externals—even the self. In fact, the assumption of individuality is the source of man's sorrow. The craving for individuality, either through the avoidance of pain or the pursuit of pleasure, is the source of man's ills. The fuel that feeds the flame of self-assertion is desire. Salvation (*gedatsu*) is breaking the bonds of this desire that binds one to life processes; it is escape from finitude and particularization. There must be a progressive abandonment of the sense of individuality until it is blown out in the ineffable state of *nirvana,* the de-spirited place. Nirvana is the complete dissolution of phenomenal personality. It is ontological nihilism.

Such denigration of individual man would have found little acceptance in Shinto-oriented Japan, but Indian ideas had already been altered in China by a translation of key terms into Taoist symbols. Furthermore, transcendental ideas were unmanageable to the Japanese, for their language had no symbols to express them. When necessary they simply adopted Chinese philosophical words into their vocabulary. Thus the outward forms of Buddhism—the arts, architecture, ritual—were quickly absorbed, but genuine Buddhist philosophy took centuries to sink into Japanese thinking. And just as China changed primitive Indian Buddhism to make it compatible with Chinese sentiment, so Japan changed Chinese Buddhism to make it conform to the needs of Japanese society. Some parts could be adapted usefully. Tender consideration for all sentient beings (for they all share the Buddha nature), an acceptance of life's miseries, a realization of the ephemeral nature of life, which allows one with poignant resignation to part with life's cherished moments or things—all these ideas helped the Japanese towards his goal of a life in harmony with nature and man. Individualism, in the Japanese view, easily led to anarchy and could destroy a nation. Thus in such a conservative, emperor-oriented, communal cult society, the Buddhist de-emphasis of the individual in the interest of the group could be greatly utilized and was. It is a recurring theme in Japan, influencing the thought even of those who eschew Buddhism. Fukuzawa Yukichi (1835-1901), a leading thinker during the Meiji Restoration, attempted to break with Japan's religious past in laying down an ideological basis for modern Japan, but even he could not divest himself of this depersonalizing tendency in Buddhism. Fukuzawa followed Chu Hsi's concept of a universe the guiding principle of which was not a Creator but the impersonal *li*. He took an extremely pessimistic view of man, calling him a maggot (*ujimushi*) crawling over the face of the globe, a small insignificant creature, hopelessly lost within the vast cosmic machine. Since the Pacific War the Japanese individual has been largely emancipated, but the age-old Buddhist pejorative view of man's personality is still evident in the social pressures for uniformity in life-style that mark Japan today and in such things as a strong emphasis on group participation. The Japanese individual as such has no clearly defined purpose or place. Not that Buddhism is having this effect by its teachings per se. For the most part, Japanese youth are estranged from all religion and very seldom visit the temples. Depersonalization goes on within thought and language patterns. The Japanese language, with its characteristic absence of pronouns, tends to submerge the individual into his environment. For instance, the experience of loneliness is expressed in English as, "I am lonely." Japanese renders the same thought with a single adjective, *sabishii*. That is, to the Japanese the whole setting is one of loneliness—the scene, he himself, and his listener are caught up into an experience of loneliness. This depersonalization is further revealed in the way the Japanese make decisions, decisions which again, in each generation, elevate groups, clubs, organizations, and family at the expense of the individual. Seldom will the individual himself be decisive and pioneering. It must be the group. And no matter how active and successful this group may be, the problem of the estrangement of the self is left unsolved.

THE JAPANESE IN SOCIETY

Buddhism lost man during Japan's dark ages (the fourteenth and sixteenth centuries), but during the Tokugawa period (1600-1867) Confucianism found him again—within a social nexus. For Shinto, man's ultimate concern is to merge with nature; for Confucianism it is to merge with society. Whereas faith in a transcendental God leads to universalism, private enterprise, and personality development in culture, faith in an earthly master leads to particularism and a concern with political values and the integrative functions of culture. This emphasis on political values and social integration was the essence of Tokugawa Neo-Confucianism; it gave a religious dimension to Tokugawa ethics, so that self-cultivation, frugality, and hard work could be utilized for clan goals. Acts of gratitude to the divine *kami* were to be performed toward one's superiors. In this sense religion diverted revolutionary energy into constructive national goals during the Meiji period (1868 1912). Sublimation of petty goals to national preservation and identity enabled the Japanese to modernize quickly.

Today, this view of man's role in society manifests itself in the Japanese preoccupation with obligation—the *on* or *hoon,* terms which express obligation and duty to return favors received from parents, ancestors, or friends. The entire society is structured along a debit and credit system. From top to bottom an unseen hierarchy exists, knit together tightly by obligation, responsibility, duty, favor. Society becomes an ultimate concern, as Hori Ichiro asserts:

> The Japanese social structure and value system took the shape of a human relationship which is strictly controlled and regulated by the patriarch according to the status of each member of the family. However, the patriarch, in turn, must be responsible to the higher authorities of the nation at large as well as to his ancestors. Even the emperor himself is responsible to his ancestors for his behavior and must account to them. In the Japanese way of thinking which emerged from the context of such a value system, there could be no room to develop the concept of an "Almighty God."[6]

Japanese youth are breaking loose from these bothersome nets of obligation. But their new freedom is only apparent. They leave the family only to be snagged in a factory nexus. Of course, rural Japan still adheres to the *Gemeinschaft* societal pattern of the extended family. People do not join a *Gemeinschaft* society; they are born into it. It is a communal society with no surplus people, for each has his task to perform. This is the traditional pattern of pre-war Japan, a carry-over from Tokugawa Confucian society. However, the family bonds are not as stringent—the father is no longer the source of unquestioned authority. In urban Japan the *Gesellschaft* social pattern of voluntary association has emerged. Participation in the *Gesellschaft* society is based on the rational pursuit of self-interest. The basic unit is the nuclear family of father, mother, and children; grandparents live elsewhere. But the *Gesellschaft* society of urban Japan with its depersonalized apartment-house living has created a new sense of alienation. Thus, to find identity Japanese are returning to a communal-type society—this time within the structures of business and industry. The social nexus, whether family or factory, is still an ultimate concern. And this Tokugawa legacy of finding identity in relationships has produced four characteristics in the Japanese character. First, the Japanese tend to become passive and submissive

[6] Hori Ichiro, "Appearance of Individual Consciousness," *The Japanese Mind,* ed. Charles Moore, East West Center Press, Honolulu, 1967, p. 203.

before a group; they are often content to "do nothing but accept with a slavish docility that which is taught by the governing authorities."[7] True, the present-day student unrest, with its sometimes violent rebellion against school authorities, seems to contradict this. But when one singles out a student participating in such demonstrations, he finds that those actions can be traced not so much to private judgment based on personal inquiry as to peer-group pressures on campus. "Because my club is doing it" is sufficient reason. Secondly, Confucianism has contributed to the Japanese concept of righteousness. The rightness or wrongness of an act is determined by those around whom one's life is ordered. Hence the keen Japanese sensitivity to the feelings, to the approval or disapproval, of others. Righteousness is a horizontal concept tantamount to right relationships. Thirdly, the whole complex network of social obligations, which are often indeterminate, produces a jurisprudence marked by vagueness and confusion. Kawashima Takeyoshi explains:

> In view of such an image of the individual, there is lacking the antithesis between the actual social world and legal rules which is characteristic of Western society. Given such an image, law is not expected to function with the precision of a machine. A lawsuit, which in its nature makes distinctions between right and wrong, is in contradiction to the social order, based on diffusely defined indeterminate social obligations; hence it is undesirable; and mediation is the means which fits the indeterminate social order.[8]

And lastly, this emphasis on social nexus leads to an inordinate dependency on others. The Japanese word which expresses this is *amaeru.* Richard K. Beardsley discusses its meaning:

[7] Furukawa Tesshi, "The Individual in Japanese Ethics," *The Japanese Mind,* p. 239.

[8] Kawashima Takeyoshi, "The Individual in Law and Order," *The Japanese Mind,* pp. 274-275.

> . . . Depending on context, the verb *amaeru* denotes "to be cuddlesome, coquettish, lovable; to act like a spoiled child; to take advantage (of someone)." . . . Whether the attitude invites love (by being cuddlesome), selfishly demands attention (by acting spoiled), or feeds on another person (by taking advantage), Doi Takeo, the psychologist, believes its central meaning refers to dependency needs.[9]

From one's childhood and the doting of his mother, through school, into the business structures, and throughout life, this desire to be *amaeru* is pervasive.

THE JAPANESE LIFE GOAL

Shinto and Confucianism have given us the Japanese view of man; he is in the cosmos, at harmony with nature and with his fellow man. But what about man's life goal? During the Meiji era, Japanese intellectuals learned about man's life goal from Western philosophers such as Spencer, Hume, Locke and Hegel. Ideas about the inevitability of progress, the essential goodness of man, ethics as open to investigation by the same procedure that unlocks nature's secrets—these ideas fixed the Japanese goal. The utilitarianism of Fukuzawa Yukichi triumphed as the ideological control for pursuing these humanistic goals. Everything, including religion and ethics, is subservient to the one supreme goal of a happy life. If religion helps, use it; if not, discard it. Reischauer calls the Japanese "goal-oriented," the Chinese "status-oriented."[10] Both traditions see man in a continuum with nature. The Chinese man and the Japanese man alike are cosmopolitan, citizens of the cosmos. But with this difference: in China man scales hierarchal structures with ladders of learning, party activity, work achievement, and social involvement; in

[9] Richard K. Beardsley, "Personality Psychology," *Twelve Doors to Japan*, McGraw-Hill Book Company, New York, 1965, p. 377.

[10] Fairbank, *East Asia: The Modern Transformation*, p. 181.

Japan man seeks fulfillment in the home or firm. It is true that the Japanese man once found self-fulfillment in the lord-vassal relationship, but this relationship was greatly weakened by Western utilitarianism as championed by Fukuzawa. Later the Japanese man found self-fulfillment in the emperor-subject relationship, but that, of course, ended in bitter disappointment. He has returned for the time being to the confines of his home. No national goal or purpose has been articulated by contemporary Japanese leadership, and until that time comes, Japanese goals, dynamics for living, and ethics will be family-oriented. Existentialism appealed to intellectuals in post-war Japan, where traditional values had been shattered. From 1945 to 1955 it had the grey color of nihilism, but with rising prosperity existentialism has assumed the gaudy tones of pleasure: eat, drink, and be merry. National goals fade before the brighter prospect of leisure.

JAPANESE SOCIAL REFORM

Have these ideas brought about social reform? The modern period begins with the demise of the military "tent" government (*bakufu*, 1600-1867) of the powerful Tokugawa line of generalissimos (*shogun*) and the restoration of Emperor Meiji as the legitimate ruler of Japan in 1868. By then, the man-in-the-cosmos ethos had unquestionably developed a unique culture on the Japanese islands. Primitive Shinto beliefs about man's oneness with nature found expression in the beautiful thirty-one-syllable *waka* and seventeen-syllable *haiku* poetry. These were essentially nature poems, depicting nature simply and poignantly. After the coming of Buddhist culture in the Nara-Heian periods (710-1159), Japanese poets began to sense the relation of the macrocosm to their personal lives. The fleeting course of nature became a vivid metaphor of the transitoriness of court life with its tragic vicissitudes.

Zen Buddhism during the Ashikaga period (1336-1573) had a profound influence on Japanese culture. By eliminating the dichotomy between life and death, by stressing resoluteness in breaking through the enemy's ranks as one breaks through to the enlightenment, Zen provided a philosophical basis for the Japanese Code of the Warrior (*bushido*). Zen also contributed to the development of a distinctive Japanese architecture. Simple, airy, natural wood rooms with mat floors brought nature into one's life as guest, not as intruder. Brush painting (*sumie*) and realistic art (*chunzō*) trace their foundations to Zen: "By restricting themselves to the simplest and most elemental of materials, the painters reflected the manner by which the philosophical tradition in Zen Buddhism saw a fundamental, unifying core of reality, eternal and incorruptible within the complexity of the phenomenal everyday world."[11]

Confucianism, with its stress on relationships and proper role-playing, did much to structure a compact, class-conscious Tokugawa society impervious to external stimuli. Some of the more energetic Tokugawa leaders attempted agricultural and economic reforms, but these were makeshift repairs at best. A ruling class whose privileges and perquisites were built upon feudalism could hardly be expected to be receptive to reforms radical enough to topple that feudal structure. In fact, no one within the system questioned the basic pattern of Tokugawa society or its class morality. In Edwin Reischauer's words, "It took a strong blow from outside Japan to shake its political structure and reveal how weak its economic and social foundations had become, and how unreliable its ideological supports."[12]

11 Noma Seiroku, *The Arts of Japan, Ancient and Medieval,* tr. John Rosefield, Kodansha International, Tokyo, 1966, p. 189.

12 Reischauer, *East Asia: The Great Tradition,* p. 668.

Early Western Contacts with Japan

Westerners had already arrived in Japan before the modern period began. Portuguese sailors came ashore on Tanegashima in Southern Kyushu in 1543. The Jesuit missionary Francis Xavier and his group arrived in 1549. Though eventually Xavier found himself standing before the powerful Japanese barons (*daimyo*) and their retainers denouncing idolatry, sodomy, and abortion, he was in the main very favorably impressed with the Japanese people. He wrote: "I think among barbarous nations there can be none that has more natural goodness than Japan."[13] The Japanese, in turn, were remarkably receptive to his preaching. Xavier's band was even more favorably received on Hirado Island, future headquarters for Portuguese merchants. The work proceeding better than his fondest hopes, Xavier went afoot in the deep of winter to Kyoto for an audience with the emperor. But the capital was torn by the ravages of civil war, and the only way to the emperor was by paying exorbitant bribes to unscrupulous *daimyo*. Thus thwarted in his strategic mission, Xavier left Japan in 1551.

After 1563, sensing that Catholicism would abet their purposes of developing trade and thwarting the Buddhist clergy, several Kyushu barons professed the Catholic faith and were baptized. The investment of Jesuit labor on a few powerful *daimyo* like Ōtomo paid quick dividends. With small numbers of Japanese and foreign missionaries, Catholics founded many churches, established hospitals, and by 1582 secured 150,000 communicants. But this conquest of Japan was halted in 1596 by the inadvertent words of a Spanish seaman. Using bravado to cower bewildered Japanese, he pointed out Spain's dominions on a map produced from his shipwrecked *San Felipe*. News of this encounter

[13] Herbert Gowen, *Five Foreigners in Japan*, Fleming H. Revell Company, New York, 1936, p. 76.

stirred the powerful *shogun* Hideyoshi into action. Catholic missionaries suddenly appeared as the avant-garde of Western imperialism. So Hideyoshi ordered the deportation of all foreign priests in 1597. Christianity became proscribed, twenty-six martyrs were crucified in Nagasaki, and each year the Japanese were required to go through a disavowal ceremony of trampling on a picture of Christ or Mary. The persecution finally spent itself in the terrible slaughter of Christian peasants at the Shimabara Revolt in 1638. Japan then entered a self-imposed isolation which lasted over 200 years.

But alien ideas continued to trickle in through Chinese merchantmen plying Japan's waters, through the trade going to Korea via the Ryukyus, and from the Dutch colony on Deshima off Nagasaki. The Dutch were permitted to remain on Deshima because of the nonreligious character of their enterprise (in fact, they had furnished artillery support in the suppression of the Christian peasants' rebellion at Shimabara). However, they were called time and again to demonstrate fealty to the Tokugawa court, often in humiliating ways. Each year the Dutch factory director dutifully travelled to old Tokyo (Yedo) and reported on events in the West. One such official, Kaempfer, related this ludicrous scene in 1691:

> Having waited here upwards of an hour, and the Emperor having in the meanwhile seated himself in the hall of audience, Sino Cami and the two Commissioners came in and conducted our Resident into the Emperor's presence leaving us behind. As soon as he came thither, they cry'd aloud Hollanda Captain, which was the signal for him to draw near, and make his obeisances. Accordingly he crawled on his hands and knees, to a place shew'd him, between the presents rang'd in due order on one side, and the place, where the Emperor sat, on the other, and then kneeling, he bow'd his forehead quite down to the ground, and so crawl'd backwards like a crab, without uttering one single word.
>
> Then to end the entertainment properly, he order'd us to

> take off our Cappa, or Cloak, being our Garment of Ceremony, then to stand upright, then he might have a full view of us; again to walk, to stand still, to compliment each other, to dance, to jump, to play the drunkard, to speak broken Japanese, to read Dutch, to paint, to sing, to put our cloaks on and off. Meanwhile we obey'd the Emperor's commands in the best manner we could. I join'd to my dance a love-song in High German. In this manner, and with innumerable such other apish tricks we must suffer ourselves to contribute to the Emperor's and the Court's diversion.[14]

At these times maps, illustrated books, and scientific works were presented. But such books and knowledge were kept within a very small circle. The flow of Western information into Japan had virtually stopped. In 1632, a Tokugawa decree banned Jesuit works translated in China (by Ricci and others) from entering Japan. Frequent searches were made of Chinese vessels entering Japanese ports. Books aboard were read, and if even a veiled allusion to Christianity—for example, such expressions as "Lord of Heaven"—were discovered, ship and crew would be quarantined.

Tokugawa Yoshimune relaxed official censorship in 1720 by ordering books on mathematics, astronomy, and science put into circulation. And in 1741 Noro Genji and Aoki Konyo were officially commissioned to learn the Dutch language. By 1750 Noro managed to compile his Dutch-Japanese explanations of Dutch botany. Aoki completed his Dutch-Japanese dictionary in 1758. Others joined these students of Dutch learning. Inevitably, this brought disenchantment with Chinese learning, as its comprehensive theories were shattered by empirical facts. Sugita Gempaku (1733-1817) relates the following experience as a witness to an autopsy performed by a pariah (*eta*) in Nagasaki:

14 Donald Keene, *The Japanese Discovery of Europe,* Routledge and Kegan Paul, Ltd., London, 1952, p. 8.

> The dissections which had taken place up to this time had been left to the *eta,* who would point to a certain part he had cut and inform the spectators that it was the lungs, or that another part was the kidneys. Those who had witnessed these performances would go away convinced that they had seen all there was to be seen. Since, of course, the name of the organ was not written on it, the spectator would have to content himself with whatever the *eta* told him. On this day, too, the old *eta* pointed at this and that, giving them names, but there were certain parts for which he had no names, although he had always found such things in the same place in every corpse that he had ever cut up. He also remarked that none of the doctors who had previously witnessed his dissections had ever wondered what these parts were.
>
> When Ryotaku and I compared what we saw with the illustrations in the Dutch book, we discovered that everything was exactly as depicted. The six lobes and two ears of the lungs and the three lobes on the right and four lobes on the left of the kidneys, such as were always described in the old Chinese books of medicine, were not so found. The position and shape of the intestines and stomach were also quite unlike the old descriptions.[15]

The Chinese approach to human anatomy was coming under close scrutiny and not passing the test. Carmen Blacker summarizes:

> Western medicine . . . seemed to work, to work out in the brute facts of the physical world, in a way in which Chinese medicine did not. Chinese medicine, with its view of the human body as a small reflection of the universe in which all the organs had their correspondence in external nature, was certainly philosophically satisfying. A man had four limbs, for example, to correspond with the four seasons in nature, and twelve joints to correspond with the twelve months. His heart contained seven holes to correspond with the seven stars in the constellation Ursa Major, and his skeleton contained 360 bones to correspond with 360 degrees in a circle. The human

15 *Ibid.,* pp. 29, 30.

> body was thus related to the larger order of nature in a tidy and satisfying manner.[16]

Sugita Gempaku and Maeno Ryotaku were thus convinced of the superiority of Dutch anatomical findings and set about to translate *Tafel Anatomia* into Japanese. After getting permission from Yedo and the Imperial Court in Kyoto, they released this first translated Dutch work to the public. It immediately aroused much interest in Western learning.

Another progressive was Honda Toshiaki (1744-1821), who spent the greater part of his life in northern Japan. In 1801, Honda, as captain of the *Ryofu Maru,* toured the northern islands. His writings were revolutionary in character and had to be published posthumously. *Tales of the West* (*Seiki Monogatari*) and *A Secret Plan for Managing the Country* (*Keisei Hisaku*) showed a remarkable perception of the commercial and internal problems confronting eighteenth-century Japan, though Honda's solutions were highly idealistic. Among his students in Yedo, Honda inculcated a milder view toward Christianity; in fact, Christianity was the only religion in Japan that escaped his criticism. Honda deplored the cumbersome Chinese calligraphy. To him it was a retarding factor in Japanese learning:

> The European alphabet has twenty-five letters each of which may be written in eight different forms. With these letters one can describe anything in the world. Nothing could be simpler. . . . Even supposing that some man could learn them all [Chinese characters], the best that he could do would be to copy in Japan all the old Chinese stories. Rather than attempt to help the nation in this way, it would be simpler to turn to profit those resources with which Japan is naturally endowed.[17]

16 Carmen Blacker, *The Japanese Enlightenment,* Cambridge University Press, 1964, p. 15.

17 Keene, p. 184.

He acclaimed the technological advances of the West, its navigational skills, and its architectural feats. Since China was not a maritime country, Honda suggested that she be dropped as a model for Japan. Instead, Japan should be the "England of the East."

In the meantime a new nation had been born. America was moving steadily west, across the prairies and over the Rockies to the Pacific. Inevitably, such American capitalists as John Jacob Astor began to dream of trade with the Orient. There were particular reasons for America's interest in Japan. In the first place, Japan offered a strategic location to establish the coaling stations America needed for her new steamships. Then too, American seamen shipwrecked on Japan's beaches were being mistreated by the Japanese. The prying began in 1846, when James Biddle, an American naval commander, sailed into Yedo Bay with two warships. He was not, however, permitted to see Japanese authorities. Finally in Commodore Perry (1794-1858), the United States found the right man to confront Japan. Perry's goals were spelled out for him by the State Department: (1) arrange for the protection of American seamen and property, (2) obtain permission for American ships to enter Japanese ports and establish coal depots, (3) carry on trade or barter. He enlisted two vessels of war, the *Susquehanna* and *Mississippi,* and departed in 1852 for the Far East. Stopping in Hong Kong, he secured the services of Dr. S. Wells Williams, an American Board missionary, to go to Japan as chief interpreter. Perry steamed into Yokohama Bay July 8, 1853, hastened on by the grim prospects of a Russian fait accompli of the same mission. Pandemonium broke out among local inhabitants as Perry disembarked on Japanese soil with auspicious ceremony. He delivered his note to the authorities, stating his mission. Thrown into utter consternation, the Tokugawa government (*bakufu*) revealed its weakness by asking counsel of the emperor and other *daimyo*. Perry repaired to his haven on the China coast and returned in 1854 with a greater display of force. Whereupon the Treaty of Kanagawa, substantially along lines that Perry desired, was signed. It granted Americans the right to establish a consulate at Shimoda, a beautiful ship haven down the coast from Yokohama. President Pierce commissioned Townsend Harris, a wealthy New York banker and a man familiar with the Far East, as first consul-general to Japan. On the eve of the ship's Japanese landfall Harris wrote in his diary: "Conflicting emotions caused by the sight of these Japanese possessions. My future brought vividly to mind. Mental and social isolation on the one hand, and on the other are important public duties, which if properly discharged, will resound to my credit. A people almost unknown to the world is to be examined and reported on in its social, moral and political state."[18] Harris' personal conduct and patient understanding of the Japanese people improved American-Japanese relations at the grass-roots level. He frustrated all attempts of the *bakufu* to house secret agents in his consulate. Finally he was granted an audience with the *shogun* Iesada in 1857, which resulted in the Commercial Treaty of 1858, granting the American diplomatic corps the right to reside, lease property, construct buildings, employ Japanese, open other consulates, enjoy extraterritoriality, have religious freedom, and build places of Christian worship.

Confucianism and Social Reform

Japan's door was now open for cultural exchange between East and West. However, the hesitation, confusion, civil strife, and assassinations which characterized the demise of the Tokugawa government evidenced an ideological controversy raging in the minds of Japan's leaders

18 Mario Cosenza, *The Complete Journal of Townsend Harris,* Doubleday, Doran and Company, New York, 1930, p. 195.

during this cataclysmic period. How was it that Japan avoided extreme isolationism on the one hand and the indiscriminate adoption of Western ideas on the other? Reischauer gives three basic reasons for the successful and rapid modernization of Japan in contrast to the desultory attempts in China: (1) Japan's admission that she was an ethnic unity parallel to other nations, not superior to them, (2) Japan's cultural unity, which allowed changes to transpire quickly throughout the islands, in contrast to China's centralism at the bureaucratic level, and (3) the Japanese ability to sacrifice petty ambitions to overall national goals. There is one more important reason. The Japanese people from the time of the introduction of Chinese culture in the Nara-Heian periods (710-1159) have always taken a pragmatic, utilitarian attitude toward accepting foreign ideas. Buddhism and Confucianism were never adopted as ends in themselves but as means for enriching Japanese culture. They provided missing ethical ingredients for consolidating society. Zen was attractive to the warrior class in feudal Japan because it gave religious motivation for a self-abnegating, unflinching devotion to one's lord. Confucianism gave ultimate meaning to the central value system of nation and family. Shinto promised protection by the *kami* for those who pursued national ends. Thus, religion fostered cooperation with national goals. In this way a consciousness aimed at improving yet preserving Japan in her essential uniqueness came to the fore during the ideological debates of Meiji Japan. The issue was how to become Westernized without losing Japanese identity, how to borrow without the humiliation of being in debt.

The loyalist barons in southwestern Japan took a strongly conservative, anti-Western stance. Under their aegis Emperor Komei instructed the *shogun* in Yedo to repel the barbarians and refuse to sign Perry's treaty. Their argument went something like this: Japan is not ready for such free intercourse with the West. She has a great internal problem to be solved first, or else all the time-honored institutions will collapse before the onslaught of this powerful external stimulus. The Western spirit, with its scheme of values, is centered around profit, not duty. What could be more destructive to a Confucian society than this mad quest for profit? Already the merchants are vaunting themselves. Unless this trend is reversed, even the samurai will adopt the tradesman's spirit. The traditional values of honorable poverty, samurai loyalty, respect for the emperor, all of which are already at low tide among the people, will ebb even lower if the Westerners are admitted now. Yes, we need Western techniques to bolster our military defenses, but unless the old Yamato spirit is restored first, no weapons will avail against the barbarians. We must consolidate the country under the emperor system with the traditional *bushido* spirit again pervading the nation. Then Japan will be able to deal with the West on better terms. Even if we have inferior arms, we have superior spirit. The internal problem is paramount. The actions of the *bakufu* in Yedo are exacerbating this problem, not solving it. So we must deal with them, not with the West.

The conservative approach to learning was conditioned by the Neo Confucianism of Chu Hsi, twelfth-century scholar in Sung China. Its advocates (called *sonnojoi*) derived their social order from the natural structure of the universe. They defended Eastern learning vis-a-vis Western learning in the following way: There is an overall principle in nature which not only affects the constitution of matter and things but also serves as a unifying principle in society. A preoccupation with matter to the neglect of the moral principle latent within nature could jeopardize the Japanese spirit and Japanese society. The Japanese spirit holds ethical values in proper perspective and must be preserved above all else. Thus the *sonnojoi* writers were wary of

Western learning, which "knew nothing of the guiding principle of the moral life and of the nature of the Investigation of Principles, nothing of nature, and nothing of the power of the Vital Spirit in matter."[19] Ohashi Totsuan, in an anti-Western document called *Hekija Shogen,* levelled two criticisms against the West: (1) Western learning denied the essential hierarchy of the universe and (2) it denied, in various pernicious ways, the moral relation of correspondence which exists between man and nature.[20] The hierarchical order in the universe, these writers argued, is carried over to human society. There must be righteousness (*gi*) as well as profit (*ri*). The West knows only profit. Christianity destroys the Five Relationships (*gorin*). The master-vassal relation (*kunshin*) is threatened by an appeal to a transcendental authority, such as the Christian God. The father-son (*fushi*) relationship is weakened. The husband-wife (*fufu*) relation is jeopardized because Christianity frowns on concubinage, which would save the *fufu* relation if the wife is barren. More than probing into the way things work, proper learning must explore the moral essence of things. When this knowledge is properly pursued, one will discover the principle of social justice (*gi*). *Gi* indicates one's place in the hierarchy of society. Westerners are devoid of benevolence (*jin*); they cut up corpses. Chu Hsi saw centuries earlier that beyond matter (*chi*) was a pattern of things (*li*)—strands in thread, grain in bamboo, markings in jade. He devoted himself to this kind of learning, not to that which is satisfied with the apparent and superficial. Thus the purpose of learning is profound investigation. We must not exploit nature but meditate upon her until the difference between principle (*li*) and matter (*chi*) appears. Westerners are occupied with the

19 Carmen Blacker, "Ohashi Totsuan, A Study in Anti-Western Thought," *Transactions of the Asiatic Society of Japan,* Tokyo, 1959, p. 154.

20 *Ibid.,* p. 154.

muddy part of creation which lies around the pearl of *li*, the metaphysical essence beyond shapes. The so-called students of Dutch learning (*rangaku*) discover not the essence of things but merely the regularity by which things work. How then can they discover the delicate interaction of man's moral conduct with natural phenomena? Actually, when examined closer, Sakuma's maxim, "Eastern ethics, Western techniques," is fraught with difficulty. For there is no dichotomy between science and ethics. Admit a splinter of Western learning into the Japanese edifice and the whole moral structure will come crashing down. There is no difference between high and low in the West. All relationships are reduced to one—friend and friend. Warriors and merchants freely intermingle; why, even their diplomats are not loathe to engage in merchandising. They behave like avaricious traders. No, both the tree and the fruit must go. If not, Japan's moral system, "no longer natural in the sense that it was supported and justified by the behavior of the external world,"[21] would have to be rethought. Japan would have to reestablish "The whole basis of right and wrong, of political obligation, of moral social relations, of the study of history."[22] As to how Japan could fend off a technologically advanced West, Ohashi Totsuan and his school found their answer in Japanese "vigor" (*kakki*): "Fortunately, of course, the West knew nothing of the power of spirit, its most recondite military principle being that big guns vanquish small guns, so that the Japanese would have no difficulty in defeating the western intruders with their own weapons in the event of any immediate conflict."[23]

The pro-Western, "open-the-country" (*kaikoku*) faction, however, debunked this approach, maintaining that West-

21 *Ibid.*, p. 168.

22 *Ibid.*

23 Blacker, *The Japanese Enlightenment*, p. 24.

ern science (*kyuri*) was quite consistent with the principles of Chu Hsi and the Chengs. The extension of learning through the investigation of things was precisely what they too were getting at; Western learning and technology were but branches of their own Eastern learning tradition. Is it strange, they asked, that principles discovered in the East turn up in the West? As Yokoi Shonan expressed it, "The manufacture of guns and battleships depends upon the Five Elements. The various inventions which have appeared recently in the West are quite in harmony with the Ways of the Sages."[24] Tokugawa leaders espoused this *kaikoku* position, for they were closer to the international situation. The government advocated opening Japan to limited intercourse with the West with this memorandum:

> It is desirable that the government should open trade as we recommended this winter. However, it must regard as the reason for doing so not the profit it might make, but rather the fact that such a step is inevitable. . . . Its essential aim should be to do only that which it is forced into doing, rather than that it should fix its eyes on profit and thereby destroy our national laws, bringing unforeseen calamity upon us.[25]

Such was the reasoning that justified a treaty with Perry. The lessons from the 1840 Opium War in China could not be ignored. China was humiliated not because she allowed foreigners into the country but because she did not give sufficient attention to Western technology itself. Japan must invite the foreigners in to learn from them. She must avoid a head-on collision with Western powers, a confrontation that would reveal her military inferiority. During a period of limited trade Japan could adopt Western techniques and develop a military capability. When the proper time came, she could reassert

24 *Ibid.*, p. 23.

25 W. G. Beasley, *Select Documents on the Basis of Japanese Foreign Policy, 1853-1868,* University of London, London, 1955, p. 10.

herself and return to the glorious isolationism of the past. But the real threat facing Japan in the present came from the outside, and it had to be resolutely faced now.

The man who avoided the extremes of both positions was Fukuzawa Yukichi (1835-1901). Fukuzawa emerged during this crucial hour in Japanese history as the champion of a utilitarian principle that finally triumphed over competing theories. He was born January 10, 1835, into a samurai family of the Nakatsu clan in Buzen province, lower Kyushu. Though a member of the privileged warrior class, his actual circumstances were not much better than a commoner's, for his father died when Yukichi was only eighteen months old and the class itself had nothing more than a reserve status. Upon reaching manhood, Fukuzawa discovered he could engender no sympathy for either loyalist or *bakufu* positions. From his loyalist upbringing he was imbued with an anti-*bakufu,* pro-emperor spirit. But he despised the feudal traditionalism that was stifling progress in his province. The lower samurai (*ashigaru*) had to prostrate themselves when addressing a samurai of superior rank. These distinctions in rank were accepted as laws of nature. But now, Perry's arrival and his display of superior military power shocked the complacent Nakatsu clan into action. Samurai youth must be sent to Nagasaki to learn all they could from the Dutch. Fukuzawa, now nineteen, was one of those chosen to go. He seized the opportunity: "I still remember telling myself that this was the happiest day of my life. . . . and how I looked back and spat on the ground, and then walked quickly away."[26]

Fukuzawa spent several months in Nagasaki learning the Western alphabet and Western gunnery. But serious study of Dutch and Western learning commenced when he entered the Tekijuku School in Osaka, the dean of which was Ogata Koan, the foremost scholar of Dutch of the time.

26 Blacker, *The Japanese Enlightenment,* p. 4.

Under Ogata's tutelage Fukuzawa devoured every book of Western learning he could find. Fukuzawa's zeal and industry became recognized by Nakatsu clan authorities, and in 1858 he was sent to Yedo (old Tokyo) to initiate a school of Dutch learning for sons of the clan. This school finally grew into Keio University, one of the best business, economic, and medical universities in Japan today. While in Yedo, he mingled with foreign residents and discovered to his dismay that English, not Dutch, was the language of the merchants. So he devoted himself to learning English. In 1860 he got himself hired as personal servant to the captain of the *Kanrin Maru,* escort ship to the battleship *Powhattan* carrying three Japanese envoys to Washington to ratify the 1858 Commercial Treaty. In 1862 he went as official translator of a Japanese embassy to Europe.

While in England Fukuzawa took copious notes on everything he saw—insurance companies, banks, hospitals, wood-hardening processes, the party system, parliamentary procedure, etc. "For instance, when I saw a hospital, I wanted to know how it was run—who paid the running expenses; when I visited a bank I wished to learn how the money was deposited and paid out."[27] From these notes he wrote his first book, *Conditions in the West* (*Seiyo Jijo*) in 1866. One hundred fifty thousand copies sold almost immediately. Fukuzawa's style was terse and lucid. He avoided classical Chinese terms, which were ever a mark of scholarship in traditional Japan. William deBary says: "Among Confucians, Sorai had been the most proficient and forceful writer; among Buddhists, Rennyo had been most eloquent. But Fukuzawa combined Sorai and Rennyo in one style with which he proclaimed the gospel of a new civilization."[28] Within two years of this first

27 *The Autobiography of Fukuzawa Yukichi,* tr. Eichi Kiyooka, The Hokuseido Press, Tokyo, 1960, p. 134.

28 deBary, II, 116.

edition, Fukuzawa produced eight works, all designed to introduce the West to Japanese. There was *Guidebook for Travellers to the West* (*Seiyo Tabi Annai*), 1867, which explained all sorts of rudimentary facts about—"shoes and ships and sealing wax, cabbages and kings"—that were common knowledge in the West, but absolutely fascinating to the Japanese people taking their first wobbly steps in a new world. *Western Clothing, Food, Houses* (*Seiyo Isshokuju*) described with rough sketches Western food, furniture, ties, knives, forks, spoons, washbasins, and chamber pots. *Uses of Science* (*Kyurizukai*), 1868, explained common scientific principles. The genius of Fukuzawa was that he did not aim his writings at the scholarly few of Japan but at the common man. "I felt as though . . . I must try to change the whole people's way of thinking from its very foundations. Thereby I could help make Japan into a great civilized nation in the East, comparable with England in the West."[29] Another work of importance was his *Encouragement in Learning* (*Gakumon no Susume*), which came out in series from 1872 to 1876, and finally sold nearly 3,500,000 copies.

During the final clash of the loyalist-Tokugawa forces at Ueno in Yedo, Fukuzawa continued to teach the few students remaining in his classes at Keio. He kept aloof from both parties, for they symbolized to him all the ignorance and conservatism of the past. Fukuzawa carefully avoided politics during his career, able to maintain financial independence through his writings. He hinted in his autobiography, however, that as a result of provocative articles in the newspaper he founded, *Jiji Shimpo*, serious consideration was given to establishing a Japanese parliament. Through his writing in serial form in this daily newspaper, Fukuzawa's ideas continued to flow to the general public until his death in 1901.

29 Blacker, *The Japanese Enlightenment*, p. 10.

What was Fukuzawa's ideology for the new Japan? When talking of civilization, he continually used the words "independence" (*dokuritsu*) and "self-reliance" (*jiritsu*). He deplored the intellectual fetters of the feudal past but also the uncritical adaptation of everything Western. He was essentially a nationalist. Westernization or modernization was not an end in itself. Fukuzawa envisaged a new Japan, adapting Western technology for making Japan independent and self-reliant. Japan had to maintain a cautious attitude toward the West. If she lost her independent spirit, she would become warped and subservient to the West. Declared Fukuzawa:

> We want our learning independent, not licking up the lees and scum of the Westerners. We want our commerce independent, not dominated by them. We want our law independent, not held in contempt by them. We want our religion independent, not trampled underfoot by them. In short, we have made the independence of our country our lifelong objective, and all who share these aspirations with us are our friends, all who do not are our enemies.[30]

The utilitarianism of Herbert Spencer strongly influenced Fukuzawa and led to his insistence upon practical learning as opposed to what he regarded as empty learning (*kyogaku*), for example, of the Chinese Classics. Thus in theory he supported the "open-the-country" (*kaikoku*) position. However, Fukuzawa deplored the indiscriminate adoption of Western ways by the so-called "teachers of enlightenment" (*kaika sensei*). Simultaneously, he asserted that the "expel-the-barbarians" (*joi*) position was correct to a point: there must be an investigation into principles—not the nebulous *li* but laws which lead to development of inventions. Before the adaptation of Western technology, Japan must "rethink some of her most unquestioned

30 *Ibid.*, pp. 11, 12.

assumptions about the way the universe worked."[31] In essence, then, both positions were fraught with danger:

> These kaika sensei [teachers of enlightenment] . . . were fundamentally very little different from the old fanatical haters of the West. They were bringing exactly the same spirit to bear on things western as had the former advocates of joi on things Japanese. They were merely believing in the new with the same belief that they had believed in the old—with an uncritical, unquestioning acceptance which was entirely contrary to the independent, sceptical spirit of civilization.[32]

That is, he agreed with the *joi* writers that Japan must have a spirit, but parted company with them in supposing that the traditional spirit was the right one. He did not accept Sakuma's formula, "Eastern ethics, Western techniques." Japan must develop an entirely new spirit, a spirit comparable to the one which enabled the Western nations to make technological gains. This spirit he labeled not "vigor" (*kakki*) but "independence" (*dokuritsu*). Independence was the spirit of civilization to be engendered in the Japanese. "Schools, industries, armies, and navies," said Fukuzawa, "are the mere external forms of civilization. They are not difficult to produce. All that is needed is the money to pay for them. Yet, there remains something immaterial, something that cannot be seen or heard, bought or sold, lent or borrowed."[33]

For this reason Fukuzawa inveighed against the effort to discover an ideological basis in Confucian classical studies. This was a waste of time: "In the education of our samurai there was certainly dignity, refinement, and high moral principles of which they had no cause to be ashamed, and indeed in which they were far superior to the West. But in the one matter of physical laws our Confucian scholars,

31 *Ibid.*, p. xi.
32 *Ibid.*, p. 39.
33 *Ibid.*, p. 31.

despite all the learned tomes they read, knew little more than an ignorant housemaid."[34] Actually, the emphasis on relationships in a Confucian society had encouraged dependency and a false sense of security within the social framework. This militated against developing the spirit of civilization:

> Confucian civilization of the East seems to me to lack two things possessed by western civilization; science in the material sphere, and a sense of "independence" in the spiritual sphere. These important principles had been quite neglected. . . . I was convinced too that the blame for this lay with Chinese studies, so I did all in my power to base my system of education on the principles of science. Nor did I lose any opportunity for advocating the principles of independence.[35]

Traditional concepts about the union of man with nature, about the human virtues of benevolence, righteousness, and etiquette and about wisdom as being expressive of the mind of heaven—these must be rethought. Nature is ethically neutral. And yet critical, empirical learning will reveal a rational principle of civilization. Behind the world of nature lies reason, which if understood will enable man to understand himself. He will then begin to develop self-confidence and faith in himself. This will in turn produce a spirit of independence:

> In my interpretation of education, I try to be guided by the laws of nature in man and the universe, and I try to coordinate all the physical actions of human beings by the very simple laws of "number and reason." In spiritual or moral training, I regard the human being as the most sacred and responsible of all orders, unable in reason to do anything base. Therefore, in self-respect, a man cannot change his sense of humanity, his justice, his loyalty, or anything belonging to his manhood even when driven by circumstances to do so. In short, my creed is

34 *Ibid.*, p. 53.
35 *Ibid.*, p. 10.

> that a man should find his faith in independence and self respect.[36]

Since reason and progress were universal phenomena, Japan could have advanced like the West, barring the Tokugawa seclusion system. Thus the universality of progress was for Fukuzawa a face-saving concept. Japan was backward not because of inferiority, but because of obscurantist policies that hindered the exercise of reason.

Christianity and Social Reform

Japanese religion diverted revolutionary energy into constructive social reform during the Meiji era (1868-1911). First, the religious basis of Japanese society provided a rationale for modernization by channeling obligations to Shinto deities toward society. Buddhism in the form of Zen had encouraged selflessness and asceticism as an honorable way of life. Now the virtues of self-denial took the form of working late hours or the voluntary investment of earnings back into fledgling enterprises. The general character of Confucianism enabled its ethics to be transferred from a warrior milieu to a culture concerned with national interests. Bellah says, "The Restoration and the subsequent modernization of Japan must be seen first in political terms and only secondarily in economic terms."[37] Both the *kaikoku* and *joi* factions insisted they were not seeking profit; the accumulation of wealth was but a means to national glory. However, it was this very system of lord-vassal loyalties and Confucian ethics that prepared a segment of the warrior class for the message of Christianity. Why?

A peculiar phenomenon existed in Japan during this tumultuous period. Those who fought with the Choshu-

36 Fukuzawa Yukichi, p. 214.
37 Bellah, p. 185.

Satsuma clans in an effort to restore the emperor found themselves in responsible governmental positions after their victory. They channeled their loyalties, asceticism, and selflessness into the modernization of Japan. But there was a segment of samurai leaders who suddenly found themselves declassed after the Meiji Restoration. They had fought for the Tokugawa against the Choshu-Satsuma clans for the simple reason that they believed the Tokugawa would uphold the feudal structure which gave them identity, meaning, status, and goals. Max Weber has asserted that the two classes least likely to convert to Christianity in non-Christian cultures are peasants and reigning elites. Peasants are firmly wedded to traditionalism. They are tied to animism, they fear the unknown, and they eschew the unlawful. The eye of the peasant, says Weber, is turned inward, not outward. The community has taught for years what is best; peasants dare not embrace a foreign religion or ideology. Persistent resistance to Christianity also comes from those most heavily involved in social responsibility, such as the samurai of Japan. The feudal nobility, the bureaucracy, and the military are responsible to make the established order work. Tradition and its symbols establish their prerogatives to rule. Thus, on Weber's thesis the Japanese samurai would tend to reject Christianity. However, a vigorous segment of samurai in Meiji Japan had been cut off from power. They had become estranged; their hereditary rights to rule had been abolished. The destruction of Tokugawa institutions had shattered the meaningfulness of past loyalties and old achievements for them. And so these bewildered, leaderless samurai began to search for an intellectual structure that would restore their sense of identity. These men came to the Christian fold seeking salvation not from sin but from purposelessness. Thirty per cent of all converts in Meiji Japan were of samurai origin. Irwin Scheiner says in *Christian Converts and Social Protest in Meiji Japan,* "The very radicalness of the samurai revolt and the abruptness of their acceptance of Christianity demonstrate the relationship of estrangement and conversion."[38] Christianity offered them status and meaning in a shattered society. They were gripped by a new loyalty—to the Lord of Heaven. Christian ethics were high. Christian views of man implicitly call for social reform. Thus "when the samurai received Protestantism through a Confucian framework, they assumed Christianity to be the historical supplement to Confucianism. For them Christianity had historical and social relevance."[39] Confucianism to them was like Old Testament preparation for New Testament Christianity. "Christian samurai lent their strength to associate themselves with a value system that seemed to offer structural similarities to their past order."[40]

As samurai walked down this new path, they unwittingly began accepting a new theory of social relations. The division of society into four classes could find no support in the Bible. Tomeoka, one of these leaders, said, "I was impressed by the statement that the soul of the merchant and that of a *bushi* [samurai] are equal before God. The idea of such a God opened my eyes."[41] Also Christianity fostered a spirit of self-criticism, a first step toward social reform. Kishimoto Hideo points out in *Japanese Religion in the Meiji Era* that "their dissatisfaction with the Meiji government changed to criticism of the feudal remnants they still harbored within themselves . . . [and that] they then divested themselves of their samurai feelings of superiority."[42] These Christian

38 Irwin Scheiner, *Christian Converts and Social Protest in Meiji-Japan,* University of California Press, Berkeley, 1970, p. 60.

39 *Ibid.,* p. 107.

40 *Ibid.,* pp. 4, 5.

41 *Ibid.,* p. 66.

42 Kishimoto Hideo, *Japanese Religion in the Meiji Era,* tr. John F. Howes, Obunsha, Tokyo, 1956, p. 179.

samurai were the new elite of Japan, not by political enhancement but by being the elect of God, chosen to serve their fellow men out of love received from God. Thus, what began as a supplement to Confucianism became a new theory for society. They maintained that "the feudalistic morality of filial piety and loyalty must be replaced by ethics based upon mutual love and equality of human rights. True religion," they insisted, "is necessary in order to sustain new morality."[43] Another radical change in their thinking came when they discovered that they had a new Lord superior to the state or the emperor demanding their obedience. The samurai of the Satsuma-Choshu clans found status in the new Japan and simply transferred their Confucian loyalties to the emperor system. But the Christian samurai were on a collision course with the emperor system. "Ultimately, as the converts' understanding of society became totally informed by the Christian doctrine, they accepted a transcendent authority that brought them into conflict with society about them."[44] They began questioning the statist goals for which they had embraced Christianity. Society and the state existing for the individual, not the individual for society, became revolutionary ideas. Conscience not loyalty became the arbiter for assessing human behavior. In Meiji Japan there was as yet no distinction between the private realm of conscience and man's political obligations. Freedom of conscience and religion was regarded as subversive in a familial state. One's highest duty (*taigi*) was obeying government orders. Niijima Joe, another famous samurai convert, founded Japan's first Christian college (Doshisha) and instilled in his students respect for conscience as the best weapon in self-cultivation. He also implicitly challenged government-sponsored morality by encouraging private

43 Scheiner, p. 114.

44 *Ibid.*, p. 6.

education. "Christianity contributed to the tradition of moral resistance to the government," continues Scheiner, "when no real political opposition was possible, by making apolitical activities an effective means of defending the ideals of individuality. They created out of their defense of conscience an anti-institutional argument that began the apolitical tradition in Japan."[45]

The social-reform character of Christianity rallied the support of many leading statesmen. Nakamura Keiu, in his magazine *Shimbun Zasshi,* "advocated Christianity as the spiritual foundation of civilization, and as such not merely to be admitted to Japan, but also to be encouraged in any country where Western culture and institutions were already adopted."[46] In March of 1882, Itagaki Taisuke, leader of the Democratic party (*Jiyuto*), publicly asserted that Japan's three traditional religions, Shinto, Confucianism, and Buddhism were hindering Japan's national progress and professed his sympathy with Christianity. Yokoi Shonan expressed radical views in the following poem:

> The West is religiously orthodox,
> Westerners even call themselves orthodox
>
> Religious doctrine is based on a Creator,
> The people are led by commandments
>
> Virtue is encouraged,
> and evil doing is punished;
>
> Both high and low give credence to this,
> Western institutions are founded on this religious doctrine;
>
> Government and these teachings are not separated,
> The aspirations of the people are in accord with this;

45 *Ibid.*, p. 247.

46 Honda Yoichi, "Japanese Religious Beliefs," *Fifty Years of New Japan,* ed. Shigenobu Okuma, Smith, Elder and Company, London, 1909, II, 81.

In Japan there are three doctrines,
and there is nothing human spirit can rely on

Shinto and Buddhism are difficult to give credence,
Confucianism has degenerated to rhetoric and literary
embellishments

Government and doctrine manifest
The evils and confusion consequent upon this.[47]

Others suggested that Japan become a Christian country; Nakamura boldly recommended that the emperor receive baptism.

However, opposition to the serious consideration of accepting Christianity as the religio-ethical basis for Japanese society was mounted by men from the very countries that had sent out Christian missionaries. Western devotees of naturalism combatted Western supernaturalists while Japanese scholars, including Fukuzawa, looked on, eager to side with the champion. American missionary J. T. Gulick pointed out that Christianity's chief "opponent was not [the] religions and superstitions of old Japan but the skepticism of modern Europe."[48] Edward S. Morse came to Tokyo University and lectured extensively on Darwin's evolutionary theories, stating publicly that he half doubted "the value of preaching to the heathen nations doctrines that had not succeeded in producing heaven on earth in Christian countries."[49] He published *The Evolution of Animals* (*Dobutsu Shinkaron*) in 1883. In 1880 Kozu Senzaburo translated Darwin's *Descent of Man.* In 1883, J. W. Draper's *History of the Conflict between Religion and Science* was translated. Ernest Fenollosa, Professor of

47 *Japanese Thought in the Meiji Era,* ed. Kosaka Masaaki, tr. David Abosch, Obunsha, Tokyo, 1956, pp. 35-36.

48 Otis Cary, *History of Christianity in Japan,* New York, 1909, II, 143.

49 Robert Schwantes, "Christianity vs. Science, A Conflict of Ideas in Meiji Japan," *Far Eastern Quarterly,* February, 1953, p. 125.

Philosophy at Tokyo University, lectured to students on the evolution of religions based upon E. B. Tyler's *Primitive Cultures.* Alarmed, the missionaries launched a counteroffensive to stem the attack of anti-religious thought. A mathematics professor, William E. Parson, began giving public lectures on *Theory and Theism.* Dr. Henry P. Faulds publicly controverted Morse. The Rev. Joseph Cooke came for a series of lectures and told an audience of 1500 in Kyoto: "Japan cannot successfully compete with Western nations unless she equips herself as thoroughly as her rivals are equipped, not only in science, art, and industry, but in moral and religious training as well. The secret of the prosperity of the Free Nations of the Occident is Christianity."[50] J. A. Ewing of Tokyo University disagreed with his colleagues: "There is absolutely nothing in the idea of physical evolution to affect fundamental articles of Christian faith."[51] Guido Verbeck also gave extensive lectures on Christianity vis-a-vis science. However, skepticism was on the upswing. Lafacadio Hearn habitually told his students at Tokyo University "that no European scientist or philosopher of note believed any longer in Christianity."[52] Many of the important men who had entered the Christian faith under Captain Janes abandoned the ministry. The Congregational Church they had founded lost members rapidly. "By 1912, the end of the Meiji era . . . [Christianity's] chance to win official acceptance or to act as an important intellectual force had been lost."[53]

Meanwhile Fukuzawa was crystallizing his own thinking on ethics and religious philosophy, vacillating between accepting and rejecting Christianity. His basic utilitarian

50 *Ibid.*, p. 127.
51 *Ibid.*
52 *Ibid.*, p. 130.
53 *Ibid.*, p. 131.

philosophy was acting as check and balance. Once he was at the point of having his sons enter the Christian priesthood. Why? To avoid enslavement in case of a Western invasion. He later suggested that "a nominal acceptance of Christianity would give Japan a place amongst the nations."[54] Taking the lead of Hideyoshi, who had banned Christianity some three hundred years earlier, Buddhists attacked the foreign religion publicly: the presence of missionaries augurs Western imperialism. Fukuzawa reversed his earlier stance; he berated Christianity and insisted that Buddhism be preserved as the national faith. In his "Family Counselor" (*Katei Sodan*) he ridiculed Christian missionaries as mendicants. But he still had not found a basis for ethics. Unitarian missionaries attracted his attention when they espoused the idea that Japan build upon the foundations of tradition. Fukuzawa was intrigued. Even missionaries from the West sensed the importance of Japanese religion. On January 9, 1891, his rival Uchimura Kanzō, an outstanding Christian thinker, committed an act of lèse majesté at the First Higher School of Tokyo, refusing to bow before the Imperial Rescript on Education. For this offense he was dismissed from his teaching post. Japanese Christians were disloyal.

Fukuzawa reverted to the Spencerian principle of inevitable progress. Ethical principles providing the basis for society would emerge from an examination of nature and an increase in secular knowledge. Without asking how knowledge that is ethically neutral could lead to virtuous conduct, Fukuzawa pressed his utilitarian views into the field of ethics and religion. Since progress would bring changes, no set of ethical values could be permanent in society. "These writers [like Spencer and Mill] showed very plausibly that civilization was not merely a means to

[54] Raymond Hammer, *Japan's Religious Ferment,* Oxford University Press, New York, 1962, p. 87.

strength and wealth. It was a stage in man's destiny, that destiny being a continual and inevitable, if erratic, climb towards a final stage of perfect bliss and goodness unimaginable by men today."[55] If the Japanese people would pursue knowledge independently, this knowledge would yield an ethic for each generation. The spirit of independence which had in the first place produced science, wealth, and strength in the West would also promote the moral destiny of man. Japan thus would become stronger not only physically but morally as well. Ethical values could be chosen by civilized thinking men, for man is essentially good. When confronted with ethically good and bad alternatives, man will act in accordance with the good and the true.

Fukuzawa believed that this same principle of rationality would serve as a control in the family of nations. The first concepts of international law brought to Japan were those of Hugo Grotius. Relations between nations were to be based on natural law as grasped by man's reason. This view was strikingly similar to Chu Hsi's concept of the inherent goodness of human nature, a view Fukuzawa had embraced much earlier. Yet when Japan later became involved in international disputes, Fukuzawa's utilitarianism caused him to abandon such idealism; national interests militate against carrying ethical optimism into foreign relations. He stated flatly: "A nation does not come out on top because it is in the right; it is right because it has come out on top."[56] Nationalism dominated his thought. He wrote in 1882: "The one object of my life is to extend Japan's national power."[57] He saw no moral problem in initiating a war if Japan's security were threatened: "If a crisis should be at hand, one is justified in arbitrarily

55 Blacker, *The Japanese Enlightenment*, pp. 34-35.
56 *Ibid.*, p. 130.
57 *Ibid.*, p. 134.

invading his neighbor's land."[58] He strongly supported the Sino-Japanese War (1894-1895): Japan should resort to the same power politics that her Western teachers were using in China. Thus we see in the controversy over ethics and religion for the new Japan that Fukuzawa rejected supernaturalism and took the same stance he had taken in the area of learning, namely utilitarianism. This theory was actually a blend of the old with the new, for as Reischauer states: "The guiding philosophy of Meiji Japan was a natural and easy blend of the Confucian concept of the perfectibility of society through the proper ethico-political organization and leadership, and Western confidence in science as leading to unlimited progress."[59]

In the new ship of utilitarianism, Japan forged ahead of her Asian neighbors on the twin seas of learning and ethics. To provide religious symbols for Japanese ethics, she hoisted the flag of Shinto; vague Shinto myths and sentiment were formulated into a national religion. But Fukuzawa's confidence in utilitarianism proved to be misplaced. Blacker's conclusion to his study of the Japanese enlightenment hints at the difficulty: "Fukuzawa died before he could discover that the increase in scientific, ethically neutral knowledge did not lead inevitably to states of greater virtue; did not necessarily make men less unreasonable, bellicose, selfish or silly—before he could discover in fact that combined with the wrong kind of moral purpose, the techniques of science might lead away rather than towards the utopia."[60]

Missionaries and Social Reform

Though Fukuzawan principles carried the day in the Meiji period, samurai with a Christian perspective con-

58 *Ibid.*, p. 135.

59 Fairbank, p. 267.

60 Blacker, *The Japanese Enlightenment*, p. 139.

tinued to speak out on social issues and to work for social reform. One may reasonably ask, "Why this social concern?" The Bible and Christian literature were responsible for new concepts. But the application of these concepts to Japan's social problems was being carried out before Japanese eyes by a handful of missionaries. Townsend Harris, the first consul-general, initiated and urgently requested the Episcopalian mission board to send missionaries. The board dispatched the first missionary, John Liggins, from China in 1859. Liggins had gone to Nagasaki from China to recuperate from an illness, so he sensed God's leading in this concurrence of events when the appointment reached him there. C. M. Williams, another Episcopalian missionary in China, left for Japan to join him. Both men had to walk circumspectly because of the official attitude toward Christianity. Public signboards throughout the country announced:

> As to the Christian religion; since it has been forbidden, you should observe this decree firmly. Secondly: heresy is strictly forbidden. Thirdly: 200 pieces of silver will be given to an informant against a Padre (Jesuit father), 100 pieces of silver to an informant against an Irma (brother), 50 pieces of silver to an informant against a Christian. It is announced that those who obtain information against them, even though they be of the same religion, if they report their own conversion [that is, if they volunteer to forsake Christianity], they will be forgiven and their crimes will be rewarded as it is written above.[61]

Despite this official stance other Protestant missionaries began arriving—men such as Guido Verbeck, James Hepburn, and Samuel Brown. The *Japan Times* of April 20, 1959, commemorated their arrival 100 years before with the following account of their individual contributions to social reform in the Meiji era:

> Guido F. Verbeck (1830-1898) was born and reared in Holland where he was educated for the profession of civil and

[61] *The Mainichi,* 1959.

mechanical engineering. He early acquired an adequate knowledge of English, French and German, in addition to a thorough grounding in the classics and Hebrew. He was greatly stirred by an address of the famous missionary to Southeast Asia, Dr. Karl Gützlaff, and while serving as an engineer in America, heard the call to foreign mission service. After three years of theological training, he and his wife accepted an assignment to Japan, under the Foreign Mission Board of the Reformed (Dutch) Church, and arrived at Nagasaki in 1859.

It was soon recognized that Verbeck was a man of culture and integrity who was skilled as a teacher of the languages, arts and sciences. . . . While he at no time kept his purpose to proclaim the Gospel of Christ hidden, he was sought out by an increasing number of young samurai who desired to acquire new learning. In time he was made the head of a school of Western languages and science at Nagasaki. Among his students were a number of young men who later served in the Restoration government as heads of departments, cabinet members, diplomats, and even as premiers.

With the restoration of the Emperor and the removal of the capital to Tokyo, the more liberal government leaders were determined to make "education the basis of all progress." In their desperate need for wise counsel it was natural for them to turn to their teacher and friend, Verbeck, and thus after 10 years residence in Nagasaki, he was invited to the new capital. Here he was to organize a complex of schools into what was destined to become the Imperial University.

Later he also had a part in the reorganization of the Peers School and the establishment of the Peeresses School. A part of his responsibility was to recruit suitable teachers from abroad for these and other institutions, and also find experts in the various fields of knowledge as required by the government.

While much of Verbeck's service as a counselor to high officials of the government was of necessity on a confidential basis, he was later attached to the *Dai Jo Kan* and the *Genro-in* in an official capacity. Very early in his career he was asked to advise concerning treaties, and sending special embassies abroad. Thus he immediately set about the translation of the most important legal codes. . . . In 1869, he drew up a detailed plan for a great embassy of the highest imperial officials to visit the United States and Europe. This included the details of the organization, itinerary, personnel, objects, and methods of investigation. When the political situation had become sufficiently stabilized, this plan was followed by the so-called Iwakura Mission of 1871-1872, which included nine of Verbeck's former students.

The cessation of the persecution policy against the Roman Catholics in 1871, and the final lifting of the ban on Christianity in 1872, upon advice from the Iwakura embassy, were both largely due to Verbeck's protests to the highest authorities. And many of the more liberal provisions of the Imperial Constitution of 1889 were doubtless a tribute to Verbeck's painstaking efforts to commend to Japanese authorities the democratic principles of western codes. Mori Arinori, the Education Minister and father of the Japanese public school system, died as a martyr of religious liberty on the day of the promulgation of the Constitution. He owed much of his zeal and insight to Verbeck.

Along about 1870, this versatile missionary was called upon by the government to decide what language and system were to be Japan's medium of medical culture. Verbeck recommended the German system and thus the Council State adopted the German science of medicine, which has prevailed until today.

James Curtis Hepburn, M.D. (1815-1911) was an American of sturdy Scotch-Irish stock who received his education at Princeton and the University of Pennsylvania. Though a man of scientific bent and skilled as a physician and surgeon, with a great reputation as an oculist, he also was well prepared in Western classical studies and Chinese, the latter acquired as a medical missionary to China.

Dr. Hepburn and his wife landed at Kanagawa in 1859, where they resided for three years before taking up permanent residence at Yokohama. At that time there were no public hospitals, clinics, dispensaries or public health agencies in Japan. Hepburn observed that "every third person was pockmarked, and smallpox was epidemic. . . . Blindness was shockingly common . . . . sore heads were disgustingly frequent . . . . while consumption made frightful ravages, as did venereal diseases." The doctor's work was made out for him and he immediately secured the use of a Buddhist temple and opened a clinic and dispensary, which was immediately thronged with "six or eight score sufferers a day," who were "literally rotting away through neglect."

Hepburn's services were gratis and as such an altruistic spirit was practically unknown at the time, the government closed the clinic and set guards before it, so that none could enter.

After three years the Hepburns moved to Yokohama where he was able to reopen his clinic and dispensary, with an average of 6,000 to 10,000 patients a year. This became a demonstration center for methods of Western medical treatment and surgery and young men came from all over Japan to attend the Hepburn clinics and to assist him while they mastered the new medical techniques. He conducted medical classes three days a week and this was the beginning of modern medical education. As an oculist, his eye clinics were especially valuable and sight was restored to thousands of eye sufferers.

One of Dr. Hepburn's younger colleagues, Dr. J. C. Berry, organized the first School for Nurses in Japan, and was also successful in securing the reform of the Japanese penal system; thereby providing more humane treatment and better health conditions for inmates of prisons.

Dr. and Mrs. Hepburn were also active in making available the Western education which the young Japanese were seeking. Mrs. Hepburn began a school for girls which is said to have been the first of that type in Japan. This was the beginning of the Ferris Jogakuin of Yokohama.

Dr. Hepburn was closely associated with Samuel Robbins Brown (1810-1880) in educational work for boys which was the beginning of the Meiji Gakuin in Tokyo, of which Dr. Hepburn was the first president. Brown, who also arrived in 1859, had been one of the earliest Protestant educators in China. He was the founder of theological education in Japan and made a profound impression on such Japanese leaders as Uemura Masahisa, Ibuka Kajinosuke, and Okuno Masatsuna.

The primary aim which inspired Verbeck, Hepburn, and Brown to master the Japanese language was the translation of the Bible into the vernacular. As far as is known, this was not attempted by the Roman Catholic missionaries prior to the Tokugawa period. When the Protestant missionaries arrived, linguistic tools were very scanty indeed and interlanguage dictionaries were unavailable.

Eight years of intensive study of all forms of Japanese literature and speech were required to produce the first dic-

> tionary, which with its revisions, became the basis for modern lexicographical research and production of the various inter-lingual dictionaries. As a Japanese scholar said, "this provided the golden key between the East and the West," and "made neighbors of distant nations."
>
> Hepburn and Brown and their colleagues, both Japanese and foreign, were now ready to undertake the translation of the Bible from the original languages into a literary form which immediately excited the wonder and admiration of the Japanese people. The entire task required 16 years, with Hepburn laboring throughout; Brown only living to see the completion of the New Testament; and Verbeck working only on the Old Testament in the latter years. Associated with them were the Japanese scholars Matsuyama, F., Takahashi Goro and Okuno Masatsuna. Matsuyama was mainly responsible for the uniform literary excellence of the whole work.
>
> Missionaries, like Verbeck, did much to introduce and secure the translation of the best literature in all fields. Many of the text books, especially in the middle and high schools were explicitly Christian. The liberal writers, realizing that Protestant Christianity underlay Western culture, gave full place to Christian ideas. Most of the well-known and influential scholarly or critical magazines of the Meiji Era were Protestant, such as the *Rikugo Zasshi, Fukuin Shimpo, Kokumin no Tomo, Jogaku Zasshi, Bungakkai,* and *Nihon Hyoron.* Belles-Lettres were also influenced in the same way.[62]

This practical missionary involvement in Japan's social reform made a tremendous impact on young Japanese. For instance, Taihei Shonan, one of the first foreign students in America, returned from Rutgers University filled with enthusiasm for modern Japan. With Western culture and technology the new Japan would quickly rise to her place among Western nations. He prevailed upon his uncle to finance and initiate a "foreign school." Verbeck was consulted about a teacher and invited L. L. Janes to be principal. Janes accepted the challenge and quickly established a well-disciplined School of Western Learning which

62 *Japan Times,* 1959.

taught the sciences, ethics, and English. The young men who gathered around him in Kumamoto were destined to be leaders in the new Japan. For the first three years, Janes' emphasis was on moral education. "Then one day in an astronomy class, he dilated on the immensity of the universe, its perfect orderliness, and asked if this universe could have happened fortuitously; whether there was not a Being that ruled over it; and he dwelt on the naturalness, in view of the mystery, of the theistic belief."[63] This led to a weekly Bible class in his home. His prayers for Japan and the young men in his classes stirred hearts. One after another they began to believe in Christianity. But people in Kumamoto soon voiced their disapproval, and the young samurai, anguished by inner conflict, had to choose—Japan or Jesus Christ. On a winter morning in 1876, thirty-five young men made a fateful decision. They filed out of their dormitory, passed a sixteenth-century castle, left the city walls, and arrived on top of Mount Hanaoka where they knelt quietly in silent prayer. Suddenly they broke out in loud crying to God; each one joined in singing "Jesus, I my Cross have taken, all to leave and follow Thee. Destitute, despised, forsaken, Thou from hence my all shalt be." Under Kanekake Pine, they signed a "Prospectus of Faith":

> We have made up our minds to propagate this religion in the Mikado Empire and enlighten the ignorance of the people. Without learning the truths of the Bible, our people will return to ignorance and superstition. On this occasion those of us with a love for our country have been awakened. Regarding our lives, it is no concern to us if we be ground to dust. We will give ourselves to the enlightenment of the people, to justice and righteousness. This is our duty and we have come to Hanaoka to make this pledge.[64]

63 Hiromichi Kozaki, *Reminiscences of Seventy Years,* Kyobunkan, Tokyo, 1926, p. 18.

64 My translation of this Prospectus.

The most outstanding name among social reformers in modern Japan is that of Kagawa Toyohiko (1888-1960). After his formal education at mission schools, Kagawa at the age of twenty-one began working among the poor of Kobe. He lived for fifteen years in a six-by-six room in the industrial slums. Out of this experience he wrote *Psychology of the Poor,* a study which examined the causes of poverty and recommended some cures. "The slums," he said, "are a laboratory of life and of human society. From one point of view I am doing research work with the slum as my laboratory and man as my major."[65] Always dressed in the cheapest laborer's suit, he worked tirelessly to improve labor conditions. With Suzuki Bunji he founded Japan's first labor union. He also worked on behalf of Japan's forgotten peasants and assisted them in forming the All-Japan Peasants' Union.

One great reform came to Japan in the modern period unexpectedly, imposed upon her by the West following World War II. I refer to the new Japanese Constitution of 1947. In a desire to understand the thinking of the American occupation officials responsible for writing the model draft of this constitution, I asked Dr. Cyrus H. Peake, Professor Emeritus of East Asian History at Claremont Graduate School, specific questions about events leading to its final adoption after revision by the Japanese Diet. Dr. Peake served under General Whitney in the Government Section of the Supreme Command of the Allied Powers (SCAP) during those momentous early days of the occupation. The following are the questions put to Dr. Peake and his answers:[66]

> *Q:* Dr. Peake, why did the United States Department of State and the Far Eastern Commission insist on a

65 William Axling, *Toyohiko Kagawa,* Harper and Brothers, New York, 1932, p. 45.

66 Taped interview with Dr. Peake in his home, August 24, 1971, Claremont, California.

major revision of the Meiji Constitution (1889-1946) after World War II?

A: The Meiji Constitution was undemocratic. The Prussian Constitution, which served as its model, did not consider human rights to be inherent. Rights were granted by the state to the people in accordance with law. This the Japanese oligarchs liked. They found these ideas more adaptable to their needs and purposes than the democratic constitutions of France or America. They came through America but rejected the American model and went on to Europe. They found in the Prussian Constitution forms of oligarchic control they wanted—a weak parliament subordinate to the executive and the judicial also subordinate to the executive. Once back in Japan the oligarchs first established an Imperial Household Ministry, then a Privy Council, then the Cabinet, and finally the Diet. So their last act was the creation of a Diet with a very limited suffrage. The traditional place of the emperor was set up outside of constitutional restrictions. The cluster of executive offices and the cabinet were placed beyond effective Diet control.

Q: Quite similar to the old military *bakufu?*

A: Yes. The motivations of the oligarchs were not merely to appear modern. There was such a strong movement for democracy among the people that the oligarchs had to satisfy them yet stifle efforts toward genuine democracy. The Meiji Constitution was a conscious effort by the oligarchs to meet these pressures from below. They also wanted to rid Japan of extraterritoriality. They knew they could do this only after satisfying Western governments that their nationals residing in Japan could obtain justice. So motivated by pressures from within and without, they very adroitly moved along in this whole scenario of the Meiji Constitution with its facade of democracy. But they still clung to power and irresponsibly led Japan to ruin in World War II. But there came a strong movement for a liberalized constitution after the Pacific War. The Japanese people and the young bureaucrats supported the Occupation's constitutional reforms. There was also support at the other end of the line—the emperor himself wanted those changes made. But conservative leaders charged with revising the Meiji Constitution were loathe to make any fundamental changes, as SCAP discovered after five months of waiting for a draft of the new constitution.

Q: Can this mistrust of democracy by Japanese leaders be traced to a religious ideology? After all the bitter lessons of World War II why was the idea of sovereignty vested with the people still abhorrent?

A: Asian religions have no conception of an original Creator. If you are going to have the concept of any orderly universe, ruled by law, then you have to have a Legislator. God is that Legislator. Asian religions lacked that approach to the universe. When early scientists in the West discussed basic questions such as the origin of law and human rights, they came up with answers couched in God-like terms. They were religious men. If a kind, heavenly Father has created this universe and ordained that it be ruled by law, then he in his compassion will enable us to study the universe and discover these laws. In the final analysis, in the East it is rule by man; in the West it is rule by law. And the concept of law originating from a Divine Legislator is rooted in the Hebraic-Christian tradition. So when the Oriental takes a sophisticated by-product of this concept—Western constitutions—does he really understand the concept behind them? Or can he feel deeply about them if he doesn't have this matrix from which they have sprung?

Q: Is there a school of thought which believes that symbols and motivations for democratic society can only develop out of this Hebrew-Christian matrix of belief in God?

A: One such scholar, Ernest S. Griffiths, made strong statements to that effect in a 1956 symposium dealing with the cultural prerequisites for a successful democracy. Though I don't agree with all his hypotheses, he did state such things as "love for and belief in freedom is based upon belief in the sacredness of the individual as a child of God" and "The Hebrew-Christian faiths constitute a powerful matrix, a common denominator of attitudes most essential for a flourishing democracy."[67]

Q: But the men charged with drafting a new constitution, since they had grown up within a Shinto-Confucian scheme of things, could not bring themselves to see the individual as a basis for government. Their relationship to the emperor was considered inviolable. Is this correct?

A: Yes. This emperor-people relationship is summed up in the word *kokutai,* meaning national or foundational body. The word came up all the time while the constitutional revision was in progress. Japanese scholars maintained that we were changing their *kokutai,* their national body. It was the subject of long speeches and arguments by learned professors in the Diet. This *kokutai* and Shintoism are actually

67 Ernest S. Griffiths, "Cultural Prerequisites to a Successfully Functioning Democracy: A Symposium," Library of Congress, 1956, *passim.*

very elaborate, ritualistic forms of nationalism. The first emperor was not merely the founder of Japan; all Japanese are descendents from him.

Q: So, controlled by these strong feelings for *kokutai,* the conservatives made little progress in drafting a new constitution?

A: It was agreed among the Allied governments that this revision committee was to be under the guidance of the Far Eastern Commission (which included Russia). Japanese bureaucrats were to revise and democratize the Meiji Constitution. They worked on it for five months. We in the Government Section of SCAP wondered how they were getting on with it.

Q: Well, how did they do?

A: On January 31st, 1946, it was called to my attention by a man in the State Department in Tokyo that a draft of a new constitution had been published in the Mainichi newspaper. It was presumably a leak, taken from the files of the Constitution Revision committee headed by Mr. Matsumoto. He showed me a rough translation, and I saw at once how few basic changes had been made. Human rights were restricted as in the Meiji Constitution. No supremacy of the Diet. No separation of powers. It was still essentially the Meiji Constitution. I copied the translation of the draft and next morning reported to General Whitney that no progress was being made. He immediately ordered that I utilize all resources of the Government Section in order to prepare a complete translation of the draft (as it appeared in the Mainichi) and bring it back with commentaries to his office by four o'clock that afternoon. With the aid of three lawyers in the Section I was able to present the document to General Whitney that afternoon. He took it directly to General MacArthur. That was Friday afternoon, February 1st. On Monday morning, the 4th, the whole Government Section was called together by General Whitney. He said in effect, "Ladies and gentlemen, you are assembled here to form a constitutional drafting committee. You are to prepare a model draft for the new Japanese constitution." And it was to be drafted in *one week!* A number of committees were formed to work on various chapters and sections. I was appointed chairman of the committee working on the Cabinet. Another committee worked on the Diet, another on the judiciary, another on the Bill of Rights, etc.

Q: How many of you worked on that Cabinet chapter?

A: Oh, about four of us. We began to write out our ideas in longhand after getting a consensus. We wrote it clause by clause. We did take the old constitution as a model, for in theory we were revising the Meiji Constitution. We used nonlegal language.

Q: Did all the committees get their sections completed in one week?

A: Yes, in fact General Whitney presented our new model draft to the Japanese revision committee on February 13th, 1946. And they began drafting a Japanese version which in turn underwent several revisions before being introduced to the Diet in June.

Q: Did that version provide changes that would truly democratize the constitution?

A: We thought so. The Japanese committee had prepared English translations of their draft. Everything looked fine. But in good faith we never adequately checked the Japanese version before it was submitted to the Diet. That was a mistake.

Q: Why?

A: Because, as we later discovered, there were serious discrepancies between the Japanese and English texts. In the Japanese text the same old spirit of the Meiji Constitution appeared again. Whereas the English draft had placed sovereignty explicitly in the hands of the people, Japanese officials used terminology that didn't convey this sovereignty at all. They had just said "the will of the people," a very weak expression. Then when defining powers of the emperor they used the strong term—sovereignty. They had made similar changes in terminology all through the text. Our English terminology had shifted power distribution from the emperor to the Diet. But they couldn't accept this. So in spite of our explicit English version, these reactionary bureaucrats could not bring themselves around to writing a democratic constitution. Their constitution, like the old Meiji model, left sovereignty with the emperor. This could open the way again for a pre-war type of government.

Q: How did you discover these discrepancies? You couldn't read Japanese that well, could you?

A: No, but a Japanese government official passed me in the hall one day and made this remark: "Too bad you Americans don't read Japanese."

Q: Did this alert you that something was amiss?

A: Yes. I got busy and soon discovered the difference between our English version and the Japanese version. I informed General Whitney of the problem.

By that time the draft constitution was before the Diet and the difference between the two versions was widely noted. But the members of the Lower House Revision Committee hesitated to make the necessary changes until SCAP officials indicated that the changes should be made.

Q: When you discovered this discrepancy, what were your inner motivations for wanting to make those changes? Was it a case of expediency? Did you think the Japanese nation would function better if the constitution were democratized? Or did you believe that rule by the conscience of the majority was a great idea? An idea eternally true? Was it for this reason that you brought the matter to the attention of SCAP?

A: It was with me primarily an act of belief and faith that the democratic process would be advantageous for all peoples, East as well as West.

Q: Can you elaborate on what you mean by "faith"?

A: I'm not a religious man in the usual sense of the word. But I found myself in a position of being able to indirectly influence the course of Japanese history.

Q: Did you realize this at the time?

A: Yes, I realized it at the time and it gave me a profound feeling of responsibility to think that I was put in a position where I could influence the growth of democracy which would help the Japanese people. If I were a more religious man or a more humble man, I would say that God had put me there. But it was not mere chance. For more than twenty years I had studied the history and culture of China and Japan. I was prepared to act when the opportunity came.

Q: As you saw those bureaucrats coming back twice now with the same constitution worked over, I'm sure you felt first disappointment and then hostility toward them. Something built up inside you. The truth about the dignity of man made in God's image—did you feel that unless the Japanese accepted it they would be right back where they were before?

A: With me it was an article of faith. I felt I was defending the common people of Japan against their military and the oligarchs who had brought this war upon them and caused all that suffering. There they were trying to get back into power again, by leaving sovereignty with the emperor. And I couldn't help but think of the thousands of American boys who had fought and died in this war. Now we were about to lose it under the occupation. This was a terrible feeling. It filled me with a great desire to stop this from happening. The issue was over human rights and dignity. I hoped the Japanese would be able to live a fuller life.

Q: Can the central idea you held within you be traced to the Hebrew-Christian tradition?

A: That's correct. I believed then and still believe that the basic concepts of that tradition are of universal applicability as developed in Christianity, in science, in constitutional and domestic law, and the whole democratic process. This tradition first profoundly influenced the development of Western civilization and is spreading throughout the world. Over one hundred countries on all continents now have modern constitutions. Over eighty of these vest sovereignty in the people. Moreover, most of the countries of the world now recognize the principles of international law. In this indirect way, the Christian-

Hebrew tradition is influencing laws and institutions, the socio-political life and practices of an emerging world civilization.

Summary

Social and political reform was effected after the Meiji Restoration under the aegis of progressive-minded oligarchs governing the country in the emperor's name. These leaders borrowed the science and the political forms of the West. But they never really accepted the concept of human dignity nor of the state's function to promote individual freedom. Fukuzawa's utilitarianism served the state more than it did the individual and conformed to the trends of the Meiji period. National unity and collective goals, made necessary by Western pressures, accelerated the growth of nationalism. The ethics of the period were the ethics of special race (*Yamato-damashi*). Christianity helped to break down feudal distinctions, encouraged women's education, initiated prison reform, founded clinics, and established schools. But it never exerted an influence of national scope. When it nearly did so at the end of the nineteenth century, the Meiji state quickly countered with the Imperial Rescript on Education (1890), a reactionary document against Westernizing influences. This pulled up the reins on social reform in the new Japan. Japanese attempts at democracy faltered in the early thirties. After the Mukden Incident of 1931, militarists dominated one cabinet after another. When later questioned at the Tokyo war crimes tribunal, prominent Japanese leaders such as Admiral Koiso or General Tojo confessed personal misgivings about carrying out the Imperial Way (*kodo*) throughout Asia. Yet to a man they bowed to the "inevitable" and plunged the nation into war. During the Pacific War, Japanese ultimacy shaped again an indomitable samurai spirit: audacity to lunge forward against crushing obstacles, unshakable loyalty to a master, awesome thoroughness in carrying out a mission once begun, tenacity to live with small reversals while preparing for the one decisive battle. The Japanese Constitution of 1947 was drafted under the eyes of Western legal experts. This document safeguards concepts of human dignity, inalienable rights, and sovereignty vested in the people through elected representatives. However, few Japanese are aware of the ideas behind a constitution that has so enriched their daily lives. But more alarming, no voice speaks out today against a resurgent self-oriented utilitarianism, nor reminds them of how a nationalistic utilitarianism was once weighed in the balances and found wanting.

4

Dynamics for Change

EASTERN RELIGION

We must first ask ourselves why it is that Eastern philosophies—whether Hindu monism, Chinese humanism, Buddhist idealism, or Shinto naturalism—were not dynamic forces for modern social reform in Asia. The answer can be found in the relation of Eastern religious ultimacies to their societies.

Indian Religious Ultimacy and Society

We put questions about man and society to the sources of Indian religion, whose religious ultimacies range from those found within nature to those found in a point beyond the cosmos. Answers received, though depicting a final destiny as identification with an ultimacy lying beyond nature, leave man during his earthly sojourn very much enmeshed in nature, fighting it, loathing it, yet paradoxically clinging to it. On the one hand, Indian man fastens on to society and custom tenaciously because the dominance of "pure essence" has cast an aura of divinity around everything that is. This is a triumph of space over time. The essence of all that is has ultimate value and transcends time. When the status quo is divine, ordained by the gods, how can critical attitudes or thoughts of change develop? On the other hand, Indian concern with a Brahman beyond nature encourages a mystical release (*moksha*) from society. Salvation is achieved not in culture but through mysticism—final union of the self with universal Self. Human endeavor, decisive acts in history do not lead to salvation. Such emphasis creates, in Van Der Leeuw's words, a "cultural pessimism." Unlike Chinese philosophy, which remains a consistent humanism, Indian religion, by positing an ultimate religious object beyond nature but actually settling for avatars within nature, leaves man at war with himself. Enjoy life but not too much. Hate your miserable status but not completely. No decisive action can be taken. Life is but isn't. Nothing, not even you, has ultimate value. The answers received leave man with a split personality. His highest goal can be attained only when the fetters of existence are broken. Yet these fetters are so strong and binding that he must remain within them throughout life. If every social action, if every human endeavor has significance only in its ability to push man forward in his struggle for release, then the social act itself is neither laudatory nor condemnatory on humanitarian grounds. These answers received from such diverse religious objects cause one to picture India as a land of extremes—ascetic yet sensual, other-worldly yet worldly-wise, legal yet libertine.

Arthur Koestler journeyed to India as one disenchanted with the West, eager to sit at the feet of India's *gurus,* willing to participate in a life dominated by its religious concepts. He came away disillusioned by this ambivalence, this paradoxical extremism dominating Indian life. Meditation? The land of meditation was filled with interruptions and distractions. "Virtue consists in being absorbed in one's prayers in the presence of din and noise."[1] Sanitation?

> On the one hand, there is an elaborate ritual of purification practices; on the other, a notable indifference to dirty surroundings. In fact, the absolution rites are governed by religious rather than hygienic considerations, and the orthodox Hindu method of bathing is hardly what the word indicates, but a series of more or less symbolic sprinklings of the body in a prescribed order. At the other end of the scale is the deliberate neglect of the body practiced by some holy men: the traditional long, "matted" hair, grown into a solid tangle of dust and dirt, the body covered with a scaly crust. . . . It is meant to express contempt for the material body, but is often indistinguishable from morbid infatuation with filth.[2]

What about sex? This is what Koestler saw:

> . . . The Indian attitude to sex is perhaps . . . more ambivalent and paradoxical than any other nation's. On the one hand, the rigid separation of the sexes, prudishness, praise of the spiritual and physical value of continence . . . on the other hand . . . a sex-charged mythology, erotic sculptures in the temples. . . . The simultaneous shameful denial and triumphant affirmation of sex in the legends is an indication of the deep and ancient roots of Hindu ambivalence. . . . It is another example of the indifference to contradiction, of the peaceful coexistence of logical opposites, in the emotional sphere. Indians hate what they love and love what they hate.[3]

Chinese Religious Ultimacy and Society

Chinese religious ultimacy is difficult to discover. At first, the nebulous terms *tao* and *li* seem to hint at some point beyond nature, but on closer scrutiny we learn that the rational principle of the universe is found everywhere

[1] Arthur Koestler, *The Lotus and the Robot,* The Macmillan Company, New York, 1961, p. 141.

[2] *Ibid.,* pp. 138-139.

[3] *Ibid.,* pp. 136, 138.

and inside man; religious ultimacy is imbedded securely in nature. When we examine the answers received from this ultimacy concerning man and his role in society, we observe that morality is not an end in itself but a means of insuring social harmony. There is no ethical imperative standing over the individual, commanding him to right action irrespective of the social relationship. Love is graded. Status becomes important. Heaven doesn't control man; rather man coerces heaven for good or ill by his actions. The emperor's actions were once thought to have far-reaching effects upon the grain bins and the turbulence of the Yangtse River. But commencing with the Sung philosophers and culminating in modern Chinese Communist dogma, attention swung away from heaven to heaven's principle—the *li*—at work in nature and also in the society of men. The *li* is to be observed as it spontaneously manifests itself in the world of nature and in the world of man. This left man with no incentive to reduce observable natural continuity into empirical mathematical equations. The Western mind has long been accustomed to viewing the cosmos not as self-contained or self-operating but as having been created by a Divine power who now controls it from the outside, controls it by the "laws of nature." In contrast, the Chinese *t'ien* (heaven) was never truly personalized, and thus the concept of natural law never came into being. According to the Chinese world view, the harmonious interworking of all beings does not derive from the dictates of some Divine being external to themselves, but rather from the internal dictates of their own natures. Each element in the cosmos is a discrete whole, with its own dynamic, but a whole having its place in the hierarchy of wholes forming the cosmic pattern.

However, this "rational principle" of the universe could be reformulated along Marxist dialectical lines as the reason for mobilizing peasants into collectives, for nationalizing land and industry, for bringing to fruition Lao-tzu's utopian goal. But the individual, the original concern of this humanistic philosophical tradition, vanishes from the scene. Fairbank says:

> To put it another way, the supporters of individualism stressed emancipation from family domination and other outward restraints, but they seldom asserted a positive doctrine of individual rights and freedoms. . . . Nationalism took precedence over individualism and liberalism. Political movements soon arose which would again try to dominate the individual and his cultural activity.[4]

Humanism distrusts itself. The individual left to himself does not naturally emit all the graces of the *li;* rather gross selfishness, anarchy, cruelty dog him. He alone poses the threat to Chinese society; thus dominant leadership to effect changes and social progress is a must. National freedom and goals take precedence over individual freedom. Stark humanism would seem to emancipate man from all fetters, but the Chinese experiment demonstrates that man left to himself becomes a denier of his own freedom.

Japanese Religious Ultimacy and Society

Japanese ultimacy has shaped a unique person—the Japanese man. This man is (a) linked to the numinous forces of nature, (b) a part of the home-nexus, (c) this worldly, and (d) depersonalized. But what is Japanese ultimacy? Not something "out there" like Indian Pure Essence. Nor is it like the Chinese heavenly hierarchal order. A peculiar man-in-the-cosmos ethos seems to control Japanese views about any religion or philosophy. If, then, this man-in-the-cosmos ethos is Japanese ultimacy, we are speaking of something very close to earth. In fact, it

[4] Fairbank, *East Asia: The Modern Transformation,* p. 669.

would appear that Japanese ultimacy lies within man. But can we be sure? What about pervasive Japanese religious concerns? Upon close observation we notice that Japanese religious attitudes are characterized by the following:

(1) Irrational tendencies. The monism of Japanese thought, wherein discrete items, including opposites, are merged in a totality or unity called *ku,* has caused the Japanese not to accept seriously the alternative to a proposition.

(2) A tendency to compromise and to avoid any kind of confrontation. This stems from Buddhist philosophy, which stresses that opposites are apparent, not real.

(3) A tendency to avoid abstract thinking. The fact that philosophical Tendai Buddhism and esoteric Shingon failed to reach the masses indicates this aversion. Buddhism as a philosophy is a panacea for a successful life, not an escape from it. Its psychology is directed simply toward group dynamics and the elimination of conflicting desires.

(4) A separation of ethics and religion. Japanese religion concentrates on man's situation, and this is beyond the pale of right and wrong. Visitors at the colorful shrines are concerned more with ritual or cultic purification than ethical purity.

(5) A belief that truth is subjective, because the way—the Buddhist equivalent to law—is the way to self-analysis. Truth is discovered in man. What man feels becomes his test for truth.

(6) An emphasis on intuition. Zen teaches that man may achieve enlightenment in a flash of intuition, without benefit of icons, religious trappings, or dogma.

(7) A refusal to believe in absolutes. Truth is discovered neither in personality nor dogma but in an all-embracing nothingness, and all systems, whether they be Shintoist, Buddhist, or Christian, are considered manifestations of the one central truth. There can be no conflict between

religions. Eclecticism is no problem. The relative has become absolute; the absolute has become relative.

(8) An emphasis upon the group. Individual salvation smacks of ambition and desire. Individuality is seen as the source of man's ills, so his problems must be solved within a network of the group.

(9) A belief that there are no gaps between man and the divine. Men are presently in the state of *kami*-hood. The Japanese word for this is *tenjin-goitsu* (unity of heaven and man).

(10) An emphasis upon shame rather than guilt. This follows from the above premise. Before a religious object there is a sense of non-conformity or disharmony, and before peers, shame, not guilt. To be without shame is to the Japanese what to have a clear conscience is to the Westerner.

(11) A belief that religion is a means to secure material benefits. Numinous powers are called forth from the locale of the shrines to assist man in his walk through life. Buddhist escapism has changed on Japanese soil to a structuring of values. Shinto gratitude is expressed for material blessings received.

So what is at the center of Japanese religion? The estranged Japanese self resists depersonalization by erecting powerful defense mechanisms. One is "over-compensation"—making up for the loss of self by overgratification of the urge toward selfhood, that is, raising the self to an ultimate. The self has become normative law and authority. William Temple expresses the difficulty: "Value or good is therefore present in absolute form only in personal relationships. From this fact arises the uncompromising quality of obligation. . . . It is always obligatory to do one's duty, but that does not determine what the duty is."[5] Tanaka Kotaro, Japan's post-war chief justice of the supreme court, saw firsthand the effects of the self in Japanese history, and he argued that the self's penchant toward anarchy in all spheres of human endeavor disqualifies it as an ultimacy. Seeing the possibility of the self's rising again as the dominant force in Japanese life, he warned his people in trenchant tones:

> From such a standpoint, in judgments of the true, the good and the beautiful, there is no external standard at all—neither society, nor historical tradition, nor the church—but the *self* alone. . . . Such personal egocentrism has no right to sneer at the fantastic race-centrism of "all-the-world-under-one-roof-ism" which for more than a decade tried to force upon us the idea that the Japanese people were sole possessors of the truth. . . . Men of this type may not fundamentally deny the existence of God or of objective truth. But they fail to realize that their "god," their "truth," is simply the mirror of one's own self with all its inherent imperfections. . . . Deification of self makes it the victim of megalomania. Burdening the self with too great a responsibility, it leads to a spiritual breakdown, with anarchy in politics and non-churchism in religion as its final outcome. . . .[6]

RADICAL CHRISTIANITY

Lastly, we must ask ourselves why Christianity, despite its small following and its low degree of acceptance by Asian cultures, has served as a catalyst for Asian social reform. This is more surprising when we discover that Christianity is not essentially a social reform movement. To which elements within Christianity, then, can this dynamism for transforming culture be traced? They are (1) the person of Christ, (2) the Christian view of man, and (3) the Christian view of the world.

[5] William Temple, *Nature, Man and God,* The Macmillan Company, London, 1934, p. xx.

[6] deBary, ed., *Sources of the Japanese Tradition,* II, 381-382.

The Person of Christ

Christ was no revolutionary or social reformer. The New Testament documents present an obscure Nazarene walking over Judean hills, offering no panacea for improving social conditions, promising no compensation for social wrongs, teaching no economic theory, offering no divine intervention to save the day. But his character shattered the status quo—the status quo of the individual. His very presence impelled the disciples not to rise up and overthrow the establishment but rather to repent and allow God to overthrow the established self. His first concern for the downtrodden and oppressed was not that they be delivered from despots but from the tyranny of self. He talked about God's kingdom and his righteousness, not man's society or fair play. He stressed faith—not optimistic trust in a new political theory, but a dynamic surrender of the whole man to the saving acts of God. In this self-surrender man becomes a member of a living organism, a holy community, a temple of flesh and blood wherein God can dwell. Christ defined love not in symbols but in acts of mercy, forgiveness, and vicarious suffering. He spoke not of the value labor imparts to things but of man's soul and its inestimable worth. He did not explain how to existentially create values before a purposeless universe but how to relate every moment of existence to the life of God. He spoke of joy, not as a sporadic response of the mind to a pleasurable event but as an all-pervading attitude, determined by one's relationship to God. He came drinking and eating with common men, talking to them about his joy. He commanded his followers to rejoice and be exceeding glad, not because situations break nicely for the Christian, for often they do not. Rather Christian joy was to be rooted in God and his work of salvation. "It is therefore clear," said Troeltsch, "that the message of Jesus is not a program of social reform. It is rather the summons to prepare for the coming of the Kingdom of God; this preparation, however, is to take place quietly within the framework of the present world order, in a purely religious fellowship of love, with an earnest endeavor to conquer self and cultivate the Christian virtues."[7] Yet the person of Christ became a socially transforming power, for men whose characters were shaped by his became salt, light, leaven, harmless doves, wise serpents, builders, farmers, servants, investors in the world.

The Christian View of Man

Beginning in Genesis and throughout the Bible, we learn that man is created in dependence upon the Creator—he is made in the image of God. Of what this image consists the Old Testament does not explicitly state. The Reformers distilled a triad of terms from two New Testament passages—Ephesians 4:24 and Colossians 3:10—to explain the meaning of "image": man was created with true knowledge, righteousness, and holiness. These terms do not exhaust the meaning of "image," for the full image is revealed in the person of Christ, the *eikon* of the invisible God. The central meaning of the term "image," however, is clear: Man cannot exist apart from God. His acts are good or bad, true or false, authentic or inauthentic, according to their relation to God. In this relationship man achieves a psychic wholeness. Abandoning it he finds himself alone before a hostile, alien universe; he becomes a fragmented, dispossessed person. Modern existentialists understand man's being as not before God but in the world. That is, the arena where man comes to know himself, his denuded self, is the world. This is the new ultimacy—the *existenz* of being. But the answers man receives from this ultimacy are expressed in flattened, non-cubic art, anti-

[7] Ernest Troeltsch, *The Social Teaching of the Christian Churches*, tr. Olive Wyon, Allen & Unwin, London, 1950, p. 61.

hero novels, etc. The sense of alienation from society which man tragically experiences stems from a prior alienation from God. Man becomes the outsider, the stranger, the solitary self.

The Bible presents a "before God" *existenz*. When man forgets this unique *existenz* and merges into this world, he corrupts his personality. He begins to live the false life. As John Macquarrie expresses it: "Man cannot be submerged in nature or merged in the laws of the cosmos, so long as he remains true to his destiny. . . . The Creator's greatest gift to man, that of the personal 'I,' necessarily places him in analogy with God's being, at a distance from nature."[8] Thus when man abandons this "I-Thou" relationship which the "image" metaphor implies, and sets the world of nature or society as the milieu for his being, he enters the unauthentic life. It is man destroying himself. By using such terms as "the living God," and "the God of Abraham, Isaac, and Jacob," God declared that he is not the philosophers' "ground of being," "unmoved mover," "first cause," or "absolute reality." Rather, he is the God who acts in history and enters into covenants with man. The names of God are the names which speak of his relationships with men—namely the Almighty, the covenant-keeping God, the God of love, the God of mercy, etc. And because of this Creator-creature relationship it follows that man can know God. Bound up with man's very existence are the God-given qualities of faith, hope, love, justice, wisdom, and self-transcendency. Man stands at the threshold of time and eternity, in nature and beyond nature every moment of his existence.

The Bible employs various terms to describe the total living person. We shall examine the different Greek words, but in doing so we must avoid any compartmentalizing of

[8] John Macquarrie, *An Existential Theology: A Comparison of Heidegger and Bultmann,* Harper and Row, New York, 1955.

man. These terms define *modes* of man's existence as a finite creature.

First, man is *sarx* or flesh. He shares with the brutes flesh, bones, organs, and skeletal patterns. He is companion with them in the world of nature—eating, sleeping, drinking, reproducing, fighting disease. But when the Bible speaks of "living after the flesh," the flesh is to be understood existentially, as a way of being, not a substance. In the words of Macquarrie: "What makes the sarx evil is nothing intrinsic, as a Gnostic denial of the flesh, but man's choosing it as a way of life; it is choosing the creation over the Creator."[9]

Secondly, man is *soma* or body. The body is good and to be cherished by man as the instrument for carrying out the commands of the will. It can be an instrument of good or evil, but in itself is essentially good. Also the *soma* is a way of being, a way of being in the world. "When Paul says, 'Let not sin reign in your mortal bodies,' he is not thinking of tissues of bone and muscle and so on, but of man's way of being in a world where sin is possible. . . . To have a body meant to be in a world where possibilities confront one."[10] That is, there are two ways of considering the body: physically as an instrument ("I pommel my body," I Cor. 9:27) and existentially as service ("present your bodies," Rom. 12:1). As an instrument the body is substantial; as action it is existential. The New Testament usage of the word *soma* bars asceticism and a mystical withdrawal from society. A spiritualizing idealism, a romanticism, and an introvertive existentialism are all excluded by somatic anthropology. Lack of corporeality leads to a lack of historicity. The *soma* is a real entity, not merely a way of being. Thus the *soma*-concept brings to the Christian a this-worldly relevance along with an other-

[9] *Ibid.*, p. 106.
[10] *Ibid.*, p. 41.

worldly hope. The spiritual body is not merely a way of being in the world to come but is indwelt and freely controlled by the Holy Spirit now.

Thirdly, man is *psyche.* The psyche as subjective self animates the body and manages its activities. It can be considered the reflexive self or the animalistic, emotional aspect of bodily control, as opposed to the mind as the rational faculty.

Fourthly man is *nous.* He observes the correspondence between subject and object. He has the capacity of differentiation. The *nous* enables man to make deductions, to reflect over the past and project himself into the future. He can anticipate hostile events and prepare for them. This power of reflective thinking makes man something wholly other than the primates. The brutes know, but only man knows that he knows. The *noosphere,* to borrow a word from Teilhard de Chardin, is the sphere of earthly existence where reflective thought is the chief characteristic. Man alone walks in this sphere. Through his illimitable powers of thought he can transcend physical barriers and double back upon himself. And this *nous* is related to language, willing, and doing. Only with language are conceptual thought and a complex association of ideas possible. With language man has the rich interplay of symbols necessary for culture. *Nous* can also be synonymous with character, for it is the mind that directs the body into creative acts.

Fifthly, man is *pneuma* or spirit; he is aware of the holy. The *pneuma* establishes a relationship with God, thereby ennobling and fructifying all other aspects of manhood. But *pneuma,* because of sin, has lost most of its capacity for God-awareness. The Bible sees *pneuma* for all practical purposes as dead or inactive in relation to God. For this reason, though man has the capacity for worshipping God, he is incapable of reactivating himself without divine intervention. The Spirit of God activates the human *pneuma* by first calling man away from the unreal and false type of life, the life wherein he has become *depneumanized,* the life of collectivism and mass media. The Spirit summons man away from the unauthentic life, the mediocre, the depersonalized, the levelled life. Thus *pneuma* is also a way of life, the abundant life which has God at the center, in which God's Spirit empowers man to actualize his full capability. "Just as sarx meant not a substance but a way of man's being in which he is oriented to the world, to the visible and to the tangible and the temporal, so pneuma is not a substance either, but that way of being in which man is oriented to God, to the invisible and eternal."[11]

The free interplay of these Greek terms to describe man in the New Testament militates against establishing sharp divisions in man; he cannot be compartmentalized into body, soul, spirit, and mind. Man is body, is soul, is spirit, is mind. In Judaistic thought, God's Spirit (*Pneuma*) stood in juxtaposition to man's body and soul. This concept may have given credence to the popular view that man's *pneuma* stands over against his body and soul. But man cannot be so divided up. These terms are used rather in an existential way, pointing out modes of being in the world or facets of man's existence. Man has the freedom to choose which mode of being will dominate and condition the other modes. He can live where the *sarx* and its appetites dominate, or he can live on his emotions. He can live predominantly on the plane of reflection and discriminatory intellectual activity. Or he can live in the sphere of the *pneuma,* where God is at the center and all modes of being express that central, dominating concern. The Bible avoids spiritualism and animalism. That is why Christ came in the flesh. Just as sin corrupts the whole man, so the salvation of God is for the whole man.

11 *Ibid.,* p. 138.

Man is created free. Our freedom is in choice. Of course, our characters limit or define these choices, but we are still presented with choices. God can be Lord only of a subject who in personal decision acknowledges him as Lord. He wills this independence of the creature in the very same unconditional way that he wills to be Lord. Man's freedom, in the Biblical context, is most fully expressed in dependence upon the Creator and is lost in rebellion against him. Of course, such a freedom implies the possibility of real choice and this real choice can be destructive of man's true end in life or God's purpose for him. But in the best possible world (if such a term is meaningful) it could be no other way. This freedom-in-dependence is spelled out in terms of law. Law sets out the rules of this relationship. In the Genesis account of the first temptation, it was suggested to man that law was his humiliation, that he should attempt to bridge the gap between himself and the Creator, to become like the Most High. But, in fact, true freedom for man lay in accepting his dependent creatureliness. This freedom within a relationship to God delivers man from the challenging usurpers of freedom. These usurpers—be they self, pride, ambition, power, sex, or habit—beckon the human vessel on to emancipation from all fetters only to remain encamped as his new lords.

Sin in essence is the will of man to exist as his own god. It is the assumption of his own deity. Kant calls it "radical evil," Kierkegaard "inherited sinfulness," and Tillich "human estrangement from self, others, and God." It is, as Luther said, man "twisted in upon himself." It is man pressing his freedom to an extreme, asserting his selfhood to the point of rebellion. It is a falling away of man from himself, a mistaken orientation of himself away from his authentic being, a decision for the unauthentic life. It is a falling into the world, a becoming absorbed with things, a fleeing from his situation as a being with capacious powers to transcend the mundane. It is falling into collectivism, surrendering to the will of the depersonalized mass, following the crowd. To deny the Creator is to accept the creation, to make the world and its system the only sphere of life. Sin has nothing to do with the condition of the body. It has to do with relationship, a relationship to the Creator. Hence we have the Biblical words "transgression," "iniquity," "evil." It is the man who sins, not his body or his mind. Sin may find easy entry through the avenue of the body, the will may give its approval, but it is man who sins. Man in freedom could have fled from the suggestion or faced the temptation and overcome it. So the act is his, committed in freedom, and he bears the guilt. The Bible says that each man is in this sinful condition now. By nature and by choice he stands as rebel and sinner. He sees every pleasant prospect in relation to himself, not as it should be, in fulfillment in God. Thus he is unable to think without prejudice or love without self-seeking. He carefully weighs every situation not as an occasion to display the glory of God, but as one to protect or exalt his ego. Man dilutes the commands of God. He prays and performs charity not to fulfill the command of God but because he wishes to secure bargaining rights before God. He is *eritheia* (Rom. 2:7-8), a clever merchant, always seeking profit, especially in religion. He is oblivious of God's care. Every blessing accruing to him is earned, deserved. It suits him. His question is never "Why did this happen to me, undeserving as I am?" but rather "Why did it not happen sooner, come bigger and better, deserving as I am?" Sin has entered the human faculty to the extent that we can no longer recognize it. The false life has become the good life. "I do not think it is our fault," says C. S. Lewis, "that we cannot tell the real truth about ourselves; the persistent, life-long inner murmur of spite, jealousy, prurience, greed and self-complacency simply will not go into words."[12] The first step in becoming a radical Christian is to deal with one's evil nature—to recognize that hostility to God, alienation from others, and a self-consuming life-style are the fruit of indwelling sin. Christian revolution begins with personal repentance, a turning to Christ for deliverance. In that moment the Cross vanishes as symbol and appears as power—power to subdue sin.

The Christian View of the World

History

The Christian invests time with meaning by existential, creative acts. Each moment of time becomes highly significant. Spatial existence is never an ultimate; rather all life in space is challenged by time. Time is never swallowed up by space as in the cosmological tragedy of Greek thought or as in Hinduism, where history is but a repetition of the birth-death cycle. Nor does the Bible encourage man to escape from spatial existence through mysticism. Mysticism attempts to relieve the tension of space with time, but in doing so, as Tillich observed, leads man into spiritual polytheism. In contrast, the Bible maintains the tension between time and space. Time for the radical Christian cannot be evaded or transcended. Every moment is dynamic, precipitating a crisis of responsibility. Since the moment is a created gift torn from relativity and the stream of time, its contents are related to God, and whatever follows each present moment must be referred to it and derive its meaning from it. The one moment must be dynamically lived, the occasion for an encounter with God. Time is a period of fulfillment. To everything there is a right season, provided for man by God, the Lord of time.

[12] C. S. Lewis, *The Problem of Pain,* The Macmillan Company, New York, 1959, p. 48.

Man must make good use of this opportunity. Each moment, then, can be something radically new; it can cause a crisis of culture. "He creates a crisis by annihilating our acts and ourselves to make us holy and then, in union with Him, the moment assumes a dynamic, eternal dimension, whereby He can create a new act."[13] By such existential cooperation with the Lord and Giver of time, man ennobles time and makes history the unfolding of the purposes of God. Without God man's action becomes meaningless, directionless, not because life presents insurmountable barriers but because sin diverts man from God's *telos* for him. Thus what man does achieve is not traced to his own genius but to a source outside the self. Order in history, then, comes from man's exercising his freedom yet all the while mysteriously executing the purposes of God. History is not the working out of man's purposes but of God's. In one sense man is the agent throughout history, for history is the record of man's acts.

> In another sense God is the sole agent, for it is only by the working of God's providence that the operation of man's will at any given moment leads to this result and not to a different one. In one sense, again, man is the end for whose sake historical events happen, for God's purpose is man's well being; in another sense man exists merely as a means for the accomplishment of God's ends, for God has created him only in order to work out his purpose in terms of human life.[14]

Institutions then become vehicles of God's purposes, as Israel, Persia, and Rome were:

> Rome is not an eternal entity but a transient thing that has come into existence at the appropriate time in history to fulfill a certain definite function and to pass away when that func-

[13] Friedrich Gogarten, "The Crisis of Our Culture," *The Beginnings of Dialectic Theology,* ed. James Robinson, John Knox Press, Richmond, 1968, p. 286.

[14] R. G. Collingwood, *The Idea of History,* Oxford University Press, New York, 1956, p. 48.

> tion has been fulfilled. . . . The gain to history is immense because the recognition that the historical process creates its own vehicles, so that entities like Rome or England are not the presuppositions but the products of that process, is the first step towards grasping the peculiar (Christian) characteristics of history.[15]

Change

Imbued with a high sense of mission, the Christian turns to external phenomena, the created reality around him. He notices immediately that change is occurring everywhere. His habitat is changing for the worse. Given an infinite amount of time, this world will become an inhospitable, barren ball of garbage, incapable of sustaining life. Whatever he finds in the world, including his own body, naturally disintegrates, deteriorates, decays, breaks down. Eastern thinkers also noticed this phenomenon and adopted the concept of change into their philosophical systems as a fundamental law of human life. Since life is transient and ephemeral, one must not become attached to it, for such attachment becomes the source of sorrow and frustration. Man, Eastern thinkers believed, must make peace with this blind force that pulls everything with it like a raging torrent. Resisting this stream, fixing oneself like a stone in the river bed, creates disharmonious eddies and swirls in one's consciousness. Inner peace comes with disengagement from time, detachment from the world, resignation to endless change.

The Bible does not deny that nature is in flux—the flowers of the valley, the grass of the field change; the world with its fleeting fashions is like the changing scenes of a theater. However, the radical Christian does not resign himself to this situation but anchors himself upon the unchangeable realities of God himself, his Word, and his promises.

15 *Ibid.*

Moreover, he notices that change is two-directional. The dynamism of organic life triumphs over disintegrating forces. Life explodes into new spheres, from simple amoeba to complex organisms. This flinging back of the destructive forces of natural law the radical Christian traces to a supernatural activity of God himself. God has also invested man with a status-annihilating computer—the human brain. The human mind will always be stretching from the known to the unknown by deductive and inductive logic. Thus man is able to project himself into unknown situations and anticipate what will occur, as he anticipated the precise gravitational force of the moon and its whirling thrust enabling it to fling a command module back on an earthbound course. This means that no generation will ever be satisfied with itself. No matter what kind of society man establishes, with its beautiful housing, finest hospitals, or leisure worlds, he will seek to improve it, simply because the human brain will ever extend itself into new worlds and develop new ideas for human betterment. Two explanations can be given this phenomenon called "change" effected by the human mind as it plunges beyond itself: the evolutionary hypothesis of natural selection or the Biblical explanation that reflective thought is of such boundless dimension that nothing fully accounts for it except the activity of a Divine Creator.

Culture

When the radical Christian attempts to change his environment for better living, he stimulates cultural progress. And he need not hesitate: the world as he finds it is not sacrosanct. The Christian has within his ethos a potential for social transformation. His Christian dialectic of this-worldliness and other-worldliness enables him to engage in secular work freely. He does not need the approval of organized religion; whatever he does is under the scrutiny of the Judge of all the earth. Hence his activity will be continually reevaluated. And being under covenant with God, he is freed from man-imposed strictures. Just as he has an individual relationship to God, just as church life is voluntary, and just as the Bible is open for his private interpretation, so his cultural activity is volitional. In such a milieu in which the mind can run free, cultural pursuits become pleasant endeavors.

Science

The Christian ethos also produces a unique approach to empirical research. The continuity of natural law is predicated on the unchanging character of God, not on a universal impersonal law. Concepts of reality find their nexus in a Person who infuses nature and phenomena with immutable laws and principles, as trustworthy as the One who gave them to man. The promise, "While the earth remains, seedtime and harvest, and cold and heat, and summer and winter, the day and night shall not cease" is founded on his covenant. Hence there is incentive and assurance to the searcher for truth, for when he discovers basic principles inherent in phenomena, he is encountering reality. That is, the foundation of natural law in the Biblical tradition rests in a Divine Legislator. Having given natural law, God intended that man discover and understand his universe and its laws. Thus the Bible, by positing the foundation of natural law upon the immutability of God's promise, gave encouragement to the first Christian men of science, like Newton, to analyze and postulate natural law in mathematical equations. Such motivation and incentive for scientific research and private enterprise is traced by Max Weber to the Calvinistic doctrine of election. Men are chosen of God to explore nature; the performance of such works is the sign of election. However, rather than limit this motivation to one doctrine, we should trace it to the general Protestant ethos. Reformational theology developed a new appreciation and love for nature. The Middle Ages had been concerned with nature only to illustrate spiritual truths, not for scientific study. There had been a preoccupation with ancients like Hippocrates and Aristotle, and an attempt to re-create science on the basis of their data. But the Reformation brought emancipation from a sacrosanct past and a fervor for original scientific investigation: "The same independence of thought which led many botanists to throw in their lot with the spiritual reformers of their day also led them to discard many of the superstitious beliefs connected with plants."[16]

The glory of God also became the motivation for such research. Kepler (1571-1630) said, "Being priests of God to the book of nature, the astronomers ought to have in their minds not the glory of their own intellect but above anything else the glory of God."[17] Such men believed that seeking out nature's secrets and unlocking them glorifies God; hence such research was the solemn duty of every man, not just of a select few. This followed from the doctrine of the priesthood of all believers. Since the Scripture was self-evident on essential points, no one could delegate the responsibility of reading Scripture to the hierarchy. "In the same way, everybody, in principle and according to his capacities, might be a priest to the book of Creation, in defiance sometimes of the ancient authorities."[18]

Another motivation for scientific research was the Reformers' love for mankind. Since mankind would be benefited by research, it was the earnest task of travellers and

16 R. Hooykaas, "Science and Reformation," *The Protestant Ethic and Modernization,* ed. S. N. Eisenstadt, Basic Books, Inc., New York, 1968, p. 213.

17 *Ibid.,* p. 214.

18 *Ibid.,* p. 215.

sailors to report their findings. "In Holland, during the Eighty Years' War, Reformed Ministers, inspired by religious and social motives, furthered scientific schemes, especially those of value for the development of industry (windmills) and navigation. In 1588 Thomas Hood delivered lectures in London on geometry and astronomy for soldiers, artisans, and mariners."[19]

The honoring of truth wherever and however it might be found opened up new scientific frontiers. Nature's book was considered holy ground, accepted and cherished even though not fully understood. "It was sacrilege to make it [nature] comfortable to human reason, which, after the Fall, is always prone to blur and distort the facts in order to satisfy its own pride."[20] That is, a good Christian and a good scientist must both doubt their own preconceptions and acknowledge their own ignorance. Such submission to facts led to unexpected results. For example, Kepler abandoned circular orbits for ellipses. And as theories came crashing down with the new burst of empirical study, the idea of "hypothesis" developed, a suspension of judgment until experience had confirmed a supposition. Thus anyone could freely theorize about anything. The trend among the Reformers was to reduce the apparently supernatural to the natural. "Theology goes from non-wonder to wonder; science from wonder to non-wonder,"[21] was their conviction. Calvin remonstrated with those who challenged science, maintaining that truth is truth wherever found and by whomever. "If we hold the Spirit of God to be the only source of Truth, we will neither reject nor despise this truth wherever it may reveal itself."[22] The Calvinist poet Johan de Brune (1658) expressed it in this

19 *Ibid.*, p. 217.
20 *Ibid.*
21 *Ibid.*, p. 220.
22 *Ibid.*, p. 227.

way: "Wheresoever Truth may be, were it in a Turk or a Tartar, it must be cherished. . . . Let us seek the honeycomb even within the lion's mouth."[23] Thus the first supporters of Copernicus were Puritans like Thomas Digges, John Bainbridge, Henry Gellibrand, and John Wallis. Among the ten scientists who formed the original nucleus of the Royal Society, seven were decidedly Puritan. By 1663, sixty-two per cent of the members were Puritan, though Puritans constituted but a small national minority.

Society

Having made such scientific discovery, the radical Christian is impelled to use it to improve and enrich society. This brings up our last discussion. What is the attitude of the Christian as he confronts society? When a man leaves all to follow Christ, he does just that. His life henceforth must be a daily renunciation of worldly organizations, worldly pursuits, worldly criteria of the good life. He eschews "pagan society with its sensuality, superficiality, and pretentiousness; its materialism and its egoism."[24] He becomes in one sense pessimistic about society. For man without God becomes not only trapped in the cosmos but part of a world system standing in rebellion against God. The alien powers of the cosmos lead him about at will. His actions are invariably in accordance with the depersonalizing forces pitted against the purpose of God. Man without God regards himself as an object belonging to the world and regards others as the same, treating them impersonally. He becomes part of a world system wherein "every supremacy is silently suppressed, every original thought is glossed over as well-known, every

23 *Ibid.*, p. 228.

24 H. Richard Niebuhr, *Christ and Culture,* Harper and Row, New York, 1956, p. 48.

triumph is vulgarized, every mystery loses its power."[25] The more man becomes immersed in the world system, the more intense becomes his antagonism to the claims of God. He moves with the system to stamp everything flat, becoming "disinclined to tolerate independence and greatness but prone to constrain people to become as automatic as ants."[26] Of course, left alone, man may by his natural endowment and the assistance of God, the author of truth, make important medical discoveries, perform masterful operations, invent devices to aid man in his struggle against nature. But all the while, he poses a threat to society, for the sinful nature bound up with his brilliant gifts can cancel the gains in an instant. With malicious intent he can devise means of inflicting pain and suffering upon his fellow man that render the most modern society the most barbarous. Illustrations of this point are superfluous. Thus, natural man in society must be controlled by laws, and these laws must be enforced with instruments of pain.

But these laws and the state institutions which enforce them are created by man and thus open to criticism by the Christian. At its best the state is a divinely ordained instrument to check evil and promote good. Men can live without freedom but not without law. The New Testament teaches the Christian to be obedient to the state and its laws. But it is conceivable that he could obey some law only by being disobedient to God. Such a law can be resisted by testing its legality in court, by disobeying and accepting the consequences, or in extreme cases by carrying out a conspiracy of disobedience. However, the results of such organized conspiracy are often the exact opposite of what the conspirators intended. This brings up the whole phenomenon of revolution. Revolutions are mounted against existing governments when the socio-economic

25 Macquarrie, p. 91.

26 Karl Jaspers, quoted by Macquarrie, p. 94.

stress compounded by political ineptness becomes intolerable. Fiscal policies break down.[27] The discontented organize and make impossible demands. When resisted by the government, they resort to violence. If they are successful in overthrowing the government, they establish a provisional, strong-man dictatorship. People's rights, for which the revolution exists, cannot be realized until revolutionary goals are achieved. Hence, in the face of practical difficulties the reigning elite become fanatically religious and intolerant of opposition. As a result they inaugurate a reign of terror.

In the modern era Communism has espoused violence for effecting social reform. But is Communism a viable means for effecting social reform? It absolutizes culture. It posits an impersonal law—dialectical materialism—as the driving force of history. This law asserts that matter, the stuff produced by men's hands, existing in a world where men have need of it, creates tensions among men because of its assigned value and distribution. The Christian has difficulty with Communism because of its atheistic yet religious character. Since Communism makes radical demands upon all followers, it has become a modern faith by which men live, a quasi-religion whose tenets can be accepted only by making broad philosophical leaps. For instance, a propositional contradiction is comprehensible; also a tension within physical forces. But to imagine that a force leading to revolution is produced by a self-contradiction within physical matter is a great philosophical leap. Also, Communism assumes the perfectibility of man; for once the bourgeoisie are eliminated and class struggle ends, then utopia, the absence of private ownership, will appear. "Marx's classless society and the consequent disappearance

27 As developed by Crane Brinton, *The Anatomy of Revolution*, W. W. Norton and Company, New York, 1938.

of all historical tensions find their most exact precedent in the myth of the Golden Age."[28]

Another difficulty with Communism is its definition of morality. That which furthers the cause of the proletariat is considered "moral." Thus to harass, persecute, or murder reactionaries can be morally good. There is no provision for honest dissent, no provision for self-evaluation and criticism without fear of reprisal. Lenin said, "We deduce our morality from the facts and needs of the class struggle of the proletariat."[29] Communism is a form of henotheism, a faith in one god among many, because it makes a finite, closed society an object of trust and religious devotion. Questions about the meaning of life and the cause for which one lives are directed to this closed society. The society defines right and wrong; it becomes man's conscience: "When men's ultimate orientation is in their society, when it is their value center and cause, when the social more can make anything right and anything wrong; then indeed conscience is the internalized voice of society."[30] My neighbor is my fellow citizen in the closed society. Thus the Marxist can kill enemies and be ethical, for they lie outside the pale of the closed (Communist) society. But Communist goals for the improvement of life are thwarted by its own system. By resorting to violence to achieve its ends, Communism denies human personality.

The radical Christian, however, has an optimistic view of society that is founded upon a supernatural transformational potential—the Spirit of God operating in the hearts of individual men. The New Testament did not make a frontal assault on the social ills of the time—against slavery, imperialism, taxation without representation, or

28 Mircea Eliade, *Myths, Dreams, and Mysteries*, Harper and Row, New York, 1960, p. 26.

29 Quoted by H. Richard Niebuhr, *Radical Monotheism and Western Culture*, Harper and Row, New York, 1960, p. 27.

30 *Ibid.*, p. 26.

dictatorships. The early church apologetic "contains no arguments dealing either with hopes of improving the existing social situation or with any attempt to heal social ills; it is based on theology, philosophy, and ethics. It did not offer a transformed social ideal, where Divine intervention moved in to establish a social organization unattainable by human strength."[31] Rather, Jesus came addressing man as sinner, alienated from God, needing repentance. Life's meaning is to be discovered in a religious milieu. The nearest approach to an improved society is to be found in the phrase, "The kingdom of God." But this is a metaphor explaining the rule of God on earth wherein men serve God with single-minded devotion. The company of people looking in anticipation for the kingdom can be described as children of the kingdom. They are seized with a dynamic awareness of God. They are called to participate in the work of God, to demonstrate the practical love of God to the just and unjust alike. In the words of Troeltsch, "Since He is kind to just and unjust alike, so are we to be. . . . So men who are consecrated to God ought to manifest their love to friend and foe, to the good and to the bad, overcoming hostility and defiance by a generous love which will break down all barriers and awaken love in return."[32] The unqualified individualism of the New Testament taught that every man is precious in the sight of God. Thus, as the Christian community spontaneously grew in small cells, this teaching of the primacy of the individual rubbed off on pagan society. Since fellowship with God was the only criterion for admission to the Christian community, natural differences of race, trade, and political creed disappeared. "Hence the only distinctions which remain are those which characterize creative personalities of infinite worth."[33] The only theory of

[31] Troeltsch, p. 40.
[32] *Ibid.*, p. 54.
[33] *Ibid.*, p. 55.

economics was one advocating the use of one's talents in honorable trades and pursuits, providing for one's own, working with one's own hands. The Christian was not to lay up for himself earthly treasures, for such hoarding is inimical to the life of faith. Money glitters and guarantees what only God can accomplish.

However, inner preparation for the kingdom of God was to manifest itself by radical social involvement. The radical Christian is released from the bondage to the self that he might serve society according to the will of God. He is not influenced by popularity or antagonism, by a sense of personal loss or gain, but is set free to pour his unfettered body, mind, and spirit to the task given him. His life is bound up with the lives of others. It finds its meaning there, in sharing, in interpenetration with the sufferings and joys of others. This is self-fulfillment, first in God, then in others. Such a life becomes a miniature of what man's ultimate goal and direction should be. Man's ultimate goal is fellowship, wherein human individuals and God himself and his Son, Jesus Christ, are distinctively preserved yet shared. God creates us free that in this freedom we may confess him as Lord, but all to the purpose that in returning to him, he may take us to new heights of love and fellowship. This sharing of his nature infuses ours with a quality, an eternal quality, not so much in time but in its depth. Thus our life is not completely fulfilled until we stand in the presence of God himself. We need not wait but may begin sharing this fellowship now, by prayer, Bible reading, the communion of saints, active service in his cause. This life, then, becomes a preparation for that perfect life in heaven with its heightened meaning, enduring comradeship, encircling beauty, penetrating joy.

Index

Afghans 35
Agni 22
ahimsa 31, 49
Akbar 34
Allah 34
Allen, Young J. 78, 80
All-Japan Peasants' Union 141
Allness 13, 23, 24
amaeru 103, 104
Anking 75
Anyang 53
Aoki Konyo 109
aparigraha 31
Aristotle 174
Artha Shastra 31
Aryan 22, 23
ashigaru 119
Ashikaga period 106
ashramas 30
asteya 31
Astor, John J. 112
atman 23, 25, 28

Bainbridge, John 176
bakufu 105, 112, 113, 115, 119, 142
Baptists 40, 42, 44
Barnett, A. Doak 64
Beardsley, Richard K. 103
Bellah, Robert 95, 125
Benares 36, 43
Bengal 43, 44, 46, 47
Bentinck, William 38, 42
Berry, J. C. 138
Bhagavad Gita 24, 49
bhakti 24
bhuta 27
Biddle, James 112
Bihar 36
Blacker, Carmen 110, 134
Bondurant, Joan 26
Book of Heavenly Decrees and Imperial Edicts 70
Borodin, Michael 82, 90
Bose 41
brahmacarya 31
Brahman, 11, 16, 23, 24, 28, 29, 31, 151
brahman 30
Britain 35, 38
Brown, Samuel Robbins 135, 138, 139
Buckley, William 15
Buddha 40
Buddhism 17, 35, 36, 37, 51, 58, 59, 60, 95, 98, 99, 100, 101, 105, 114, 125, 129, 130, 132
Bungakkai 139
bushi 127
Bushido, 106, 115
busshin 98
Butterfield, Kenyon 87, 88
Buzen province 119

Calcutta 47
Calvin, John 175
Canton 66, 68, 70, 76
Carey, William 40, 44
Carmichael, Amy 44, 45, 46
Carrel, Alexis 18
Catholic missions 83
Central Asia 66
Chandogya Upanishad 28
Chang Chien 77
Chang Chih-tung 76
Chang Fu-liang 87
Ch'eng Hao 59, 118
Ch'eng I 59, 60, 118
chi 59, 60, 62, 116
Chia I 17
Chiang Kai-shek 81, 86, 88, 89, 90, 91, 92
Chiang, Madame 87
Chin dynasty 17, 56
Chinese Communist Party (CCP) 51, 57, 61, 81
Chinese Gordon 71
Chinese Republic 81
Ch'ing dynasty 66, 74
chin-shih 77
chin tien 64
Choshu-Satsuma 126
Chou, Duke 55
Chou-li 70, 73
Chou Tun-i 59
Christian Rural Reconstruction 90, 91
Christian Rural Service Union 88
Chu Hsi 52, 59, 60, 61, 62, 100, 115, 118, 133
chujen 77
chun-tzu 62
chunzō 106
Ciardi, John 13
Code of the Warrior 106
Comintern 82
Commercial Treaty of 1858 113, 120
Communism 58, 64, 72, 82, 86, 88, 91, 92, 93, 178, 179
Conditions in the West 120
Confucian Classics 52, 53, 58, 61, 63, 70, 122
Confucianism 51, 82, 91, 92, 101, 103, 104, 106, 113, 125, 128, 129, 130
Confucius 51, 52, 53, 54, 62, 63, 64, 65, 79, 83
Congregational Church 88, 131
Constantine 83
Constitution Revision Committee 145
Cooke, Joseph 131
Copernicus 176
Cultural Revolution 51

Dai Jo Kan 136
daimyo 107, 112
Danish 35, 41
Darwin 130
deBary, William T. 29, 120
deBrune, Johan 175
Deccan 34
Denver 81
Derozio, Henry 47
Descent of Man 130
Deshima 108
Digges, Thomas 176
dharma 17, 22, 25, 30, 32, 58
Dobutsu Shinkaron 130
Dohnavur Fellowship 46
Doi Takeo 104
dokuritsu 122, 123
Dōshisha 128
Draper, J. W. 130
Duff, Alexander 39
Duncan, Jonathan 43
Dutch 35, 108, 109, 110, 119, 120

Eastern Chou period 54
East India Company 35, 39, 40, 42
Eighty Years' War 175
eikon 162
Elements of International Law 84
Eliade, Mircea 97
Empress-dowager 79, 80
Encouragement in Learning 121
Endicott, James 91
England 90, 171
eritheia 168
eta 109
Euclid 84
Ever-Victorious Army 71
Evolution of Animals 130
Ewing, J. A. 131
Existentialism 14, 18
existenz 162, 163

fa-chia 55
Fairbank, John 157
Family Counselor 132
Far Eastern Commission 141, 145
Faulds, Henry P. 131
Fen Kuei-fen 75
Fenollosa, Ernest 130
Fitzgerald, C. P. 92
Five Elements 118
Five Relationships 52, 116
Fort Williams College 43
Four Noble Truths 36
France 35, 142
Friend of India 40, 41
Fromm, Eric 17
fufu 116
Fukuin Shimpo 139
Fukuzawa Yukichi 100, 104, 105, 119, 120, 121, 122, 125, 130, 131, 133, 134, 150
Fundamentals of Our National Polity 97
fushi 116

gaijin 98
Gakumon no Susume 121
Gandhi, Mahatma 26, 48
Ganges River 44, 47
Gautama, Siddartha 35, 36
Gaya 36
gedatsu 99
Gellibrand, Henry 176
Gemeinschaft society 102
Genro-in 136
Georgia, University of 87
Georgian principles 87
Germany 79
Gesellschaft society 102
gi 116
Goa 35
God-worshippers 70
Golden Age 179
Golden Rule 73
gorin 116
Graham, Billy 15
Grant, Charles 39, 40
Great Ultimate 59
Great Wall 56
Griffiths, Ernest S. 144
Grotius, Hugo 133
Grousset, Rene 60
Guidebook for Travellers to the West 121
Gulick, J. T. 130
Gupta period 26
guru 154
Gützlaff, Karl 136

haiku 105
hakko ichiu 97
Han dynasty 17
Hanaoka, Mount 140
Han-fei-tzu 55
Hangyang 76
Harappa culture 23
Harijan Sevak Sangh 47
Harris, Townsend 113, 135
Hart, Robert 75
Hastings, Warren 43
Hearn, Lafcadio 131
Heavenly Kingdom of Great Peace 71, 72
Hebrew-Christian tradition 143, 144, 149, 150
Hegel 104
Hekija Shogen 116
Hepburn, James 135, 137, 138, 139
Hepburn, Mrs. James 138
Hideyoshi 108, 132
Himalayan hills 35
Hindoos 42
Hindu 21, 23, 38, 39, 40
Hinduism, 21, 22, 23, 24, 25, 26, 27, 33, 34, 37, 169
Hippocrates 174
Hirado Island 107
History of the Conflict between Religions 130
Holland 135, 175
Honda Toshiaki 111, 112
Hongkong 78, 112
Honolulu 81
Hood, Thomas 175
hoon 101
Hori Ichiro 101
Howell, William 41
Hsü, Immanuel 84
Hsün-tzu 55, 56, 64
Hume 104
Hung Hsiu-ch'üan 67, 68, 70, 71, 73, 74
Hu Shih 63, 64

Ibuka Kajinosuke 138
Iesada 113
Imperial Constitution of 1889 137
Imperial Household Ministry 142
Imperial Rescript on Education 132, 150
Imperial Rescript to Soldiers and Sailors 97
Imperial University 136
Imperial Way 150
Indian National Congress 47
Indra 22
Indus basin 23
Ingham, Kenneth 46
International Missionary Council 87
Islam 26, 34, 37, 38
Israel 170
Itagaki Taisuke 129
Italy 90
Iwakura Mission 137

Jagannath 43
Jahangir 34
Jains 27, 28, 29, 49
Janes, L. L. 131, 139, 140
Japanese Constitution of 1947 141, 151
Japanese Diet 141, 142, 144, 145, 146, 147
Japanese imperialism 86, 92
Japan Times 135
Jardine, Matheson and Co. 76
Java 35
jen 55, 62
Jesuits 47, 83, 109, 135
jihad 34
Jiji Shimpo 121
jin 116
jiritsu 122
jiva 27
Jiyuto 129
Jogaku Zasshi 139
Johns, William 41
Johnson, William 87
ju 54, 55

Kaempfer 108
Kagawa Toyohiko 141
kaika sensei 122, 123
kaikoku 117, 122, 125
Kaiser-i-Hind Medal 45
kakki 117, 123
kami 16, 96, 97, 101, 114
Kanagawa 137, 159
Kanagawa, Treaty of 113
Kanekake Pine 140
K'ang Yu-wei 63, 76, 78, 79, 80
Kanrin Maru 120
Kant 167
Kapila 28
karma 21, 29
Katei Sodan 132
Kawasaki Ichiro 98
Kawashima Takeyoshi 103
Keio University 120, 121
Kepler 174, 175
Kiangsi 87, 88, 89, 90
Kiaochow 79
Kierkegaard 167
King, Martin Luther 48
Kishimoto Hideo 127
Kobe 141
Koestler, Arthur 154, 155
Koiso, Admiral 150
Kokumin no Tomo 139
kokutai 97, 144, 145
Komei, Emperor 114
Koran 34
Korea 108
Kozu Senzaburo 130
ku 98, 158
Kuang-hsü, Emperor 79
Kumamoto 140
kunshin 116
Kuomintang (KMT) 82, 88, 89
kyogaku 122
Kyoto 107, 111, 131
kyuri 118
Kyurizukai 121
Kyushu 107, 119

Lao-tzu 157
Latourette, K. S. 86
Legalist School 17, 55, 56, 57
Lenin 179
Lewis, C. S. 168
li 16, 52, 58, 59, 60, 62, 63, 73, 75, 76, 83, 100, 116, 117, 122, 155, 156, 157
Liang A-fa 69, 80
Liang Chi-ch'ao 78
Liao P'ing 63

Li Ching-fang 69
Liggins, John 135
Li Hung-chang 75, 76
Lin, Commissioner 66
Lincoln, Abraham 81
Locke 104
logos 58
London 72, 175
Long-Haired Rebels 71
Loyang 54
Luther, Martin 167

Macao 66
MacArthur, Douglas 146
Macaulay, Lord 38
Mackenzie, 80
MacQuarrie, John 163, 164
Madras 45
Madrassa 43
Mainichi 145
Manchu 68, 71, 72, 80, 81, 82, 86, 91
Mandate of Heaven 54, 73
Manu, Code of 25
Mao Tse-tung 51, 52, 53, 62, 64, 65, 81
Marathas 34, 35
Maritime Customs Service 75
Marshman, Joshua 40, 42
Martin, W. A. P. 84
Marx, Karl 178
Marxism 52, 61, 64, 156, 179
Matsuyama, F. 139
May 4th Movement of 1919 51
Meadows, Thomas 72
Meiji Constitution 142, 143, 145, 146, 147
Meiji, Emperor 105
Meiji era 16, 101, 104, 114, 125, 126, 128, 131, 134, 139
Meiji Gakuin 138
Meiji government 127
Meiji Restoration 100, 125, 126, 136, 150
Mencius 52, 55, 62, 63, 64, 75
Middle Ages 174
Middle Kingdom 66
Mikado 140
Mill, J. S. 38, 132
Mill, William 43
Milne, William 69
Mimansa School 36
Minute on Education 38
Mississippi 112
Modern Text 79
Moguls 34, 37, 39
Mohenjodaro 23
moksha 22, 23, 25, 29, 32, 36, 154
Mongols 34, 65
Mori Arinori 137
Morse, Edward S. 130, 131
Mo-tsu 55, 64
muga 17
Mukden 150
mukti 22, 29
muni 31
Muslim 37, 39, 40, 47

Nagasaki 108, 109, 119, 135, 136
Nakamura Hajime 31, 98
Nakamura Keiu 129, 130
Nakatsu clan 119, 120
Nanak 37
Nanking 71, 72, 75, 76, 87, 90
Nanking Decade 86, 92
Nara-Heian periods 98, 105, 114
National Christian Council of China (NCC) 87, 88, 90
Nationalist Party 81
Nehru, Jawaharlal 33
Neo-Confucianism 51, 58, 63, 64, 75, 83, 101, 115
Neo-Confucianists 59
Nepal 37
New Life Movement 90, 91, 92
Newman, William 49
Newton, John 173
Nihon Hyoron 139
Niijima Joe 128
The Nineteenth Century 80
nirvana 25, 36, 99
Norinaga Motoori 96
Noro Genji 109
nous 165
noosphere 165

Ogata Koan 119, 120
Ohashi Totsuan 116, 117
Okuno Masatsuna 138, 139
on 101
One Hundred Days 63, 78, 79
Opium War 62, 66, 74, 118

Osaka 119
Ōtomo 107

Pacific War 97, 100, 143, 150
Pai Shang-ti Hui 69
panin 27
Paniput, Battle of 35
Parson, William E. 131
Peake, Cyrus H. 141
Peers School 136
Peking 76, 81
Pennsylvania, University of 137
Perry, Commodore 112, 113, 114, 118, 119
Persia 170
Pierce, President 113
Pilla, Ananda 47
pneuma 165, 166
Polo, Marco 65
Ponnammal 45
Poona 43
Portuguese 35, 107
Powhattan 120
Preena 44, 45
Primitive Cultures 131
Princeton University 137
Privy Council 142
Prospectus of Faith 140
Protestantism 67, 127, 139
Prussian Constitution 142
psyche 165
Psychology of the Poor 141
Punjab 34
Puritan 176
Purusha 27

Quotations from Chairman Mao 52

rajanya 30
rangaku 117
Reformation 174
Reformed Church 136
Reformers 175
Reischauer, Edwin O. 57, 59, 104, 106, 114, 134
Rennyo 120
ri 116
Ricci, Matteo 66, 84, 109
Richard, Timothy 76, 78, 80
Rig Veda 22, 27, 30
Rikugo Zasshi 139
Rites of Chou 70, 73
Roberts, Issachar 70
Rockefeller, John 88
Rome 170, 171
Roszak, Theodore 15
Roy, M. N. 27
Roy, Rāmmohun 48
Royal Society 176
Rural Reconstruction Institute 88
Russia 82, 90, 145
Rutgers University 139
Ryofu Maru 111
Ryukyus 108

sabishii 100
Sakuma 117, 123
Sakya tribe 35
samsara 22, 28, 29, 30, 32, 36, 37
samurai 126, 127, 128
sanatana dharma 21, 25
San Felipe 107
Sankhya School 26, 28
san min chu i 81
Sanskrit 31
sarx 164, 166
sat 26
sati 38, 41, 42, 44
Satsuma-Choshu 128
sattva 27
Saturday Review 13
satya 28, 31
satyagraha 26, 49
Saugor 44
Schall von Bell, Adam 66
Scheiner, Irwin 126, 129
Scheler, Max 18
School of Western Learning 139
Scottish Churches College 39
Secret Plan for Managing the Country 111
Seiyo Isshokuju 121
Seiyo Jijo 120
Seiyo Tabi Annai 121
Self-strengthening Movement 84
Serampore 39
Serampore Mission College 41
Sermon on the Mount 49
Seva-Sadan 47
Shaftesbury 40
Shah Jahan 34
Shang dynasty 53, 54

Shanghai 75, 76, 78
Shang-ti 54, 60, 83
Shangtung 79
Shankara 27, 28, 37
Shansi 76
sharia 34
Shepherd, George 88, 89, 90, 91
Shimabara Revolt 108
Shimbun Zasshi 129
Shimoda 113
Shimonoseki Treaty 77
Shingon 158
Shintō 17, 95, 96, 97, 99, 101, 104, 105, 114, 125, 129, 130, 134, 144, 159
Shiva 24
shogun 105, 108, 113, 114
shudra 30
Shuns 53, 55
Sikhism 37
Sikhs 38, 40
Singh 40
Sino Cami 108
Sino-Japanese War 77, 134
Sivaji 34
Society for the Study of Self-strengthening 78
soma 164
sonnojoi 115, 122, 123, 125
Soochow 75
Soong Mei-ling 86
Sorai 120
Southern Baptist 70
Spain 107
Spear, Percival 32, 38, 39
Spencer, Herbert 104, 122, 132
Ssu-ma Ch'ien 65
Sugita Gempaku 11, 109
sumie 106
Sung dynasty 58, 63, 75, 78, 79, 115, 156
sunyata 37, 58
Sun Yat-sen 72, 74, 80, 81, 82, 86, 91
Supreme Command of the Allied Powers (SCAP) 141, 143, 145, 148
Susquehanna 112
Suzuki Bunji 141

Tafel Anatomia 111
T'ai-chi 59
taigi 128
Taihei Shonan 139
Taiping Rebellion 66, 71, 72, 73, 74
Taiping-t'ien-kuo 71
Taiwan 81
Taj Mahal 34
Takahashi Goro 139
Tales of the West 111
Tanaka Kotaro 160
Tanegashima 107
Tao 16, 56, 57, 60, 155
Taoism 51, 57, 58, 59, 64, 99
tapas 28
Tartar 176
Taylor, J. Hudson 83
te 55
Teilhard de Chardin, Pierre 18, 165
Tekijuku School 119
telos 170
Temple tax 42
Temple, William 159
Tendai Buddhism 158
tenjin-goitsu 159
Text Book Series Committee 84
thagi 39
Theory and Theism 131
Thistle Mountain 70
Three Ages 79
Three Character Classic 81
Three Principles 74, 81
Tibet 37
t'ien 53, 156
Tillich, Paul 16, 25, 167, 169
Tinghsien 88
Tinghsien Literary Institute 87
T'i-yung 78
Tojo, General 150
Tokugawa period 101, 105, 108, 109, 112, 113, 118, 121, 125, 126, 138
Tokugawa Religion 95
Tokugawa society 102, 106
Tokugawa Yoshimune 109
Tokyo 136, 145
Tokyo University 130, 131
Tolstoy 49
Troeltsch, Ernst 180
Tseng Kuo-fan 63, 71, 75, 76
Tsungli-yamen 75
T'ung-chih Restoration 63, 74, 75, 76

T'ung-wen Kuan 84
Turk 176
Tyagaraja, Song of 32
Tyler, E. B. 131

Uchimura Kanzō 132
Uemura Masahisa 138
Ueno 121
ujimushi 100
Unitarian missionaries 132
Upanishadic literature 23, 24, 25, 27
United States 85, 90, 91, 112, 142
United States Department of State 141, 145
Ursa Major 110
Uses of Science 121

Vaishnavite Hinduism 49
vaishya 30
Van Der Leeuw, G. 154
Van Leeuwen, Arend 33
varnas 30
Vedantic School 15, 26, 29
Vedic period 21, 22, 23, 25
Verbeck, Guido 131, 135, 136, 137, 139
Victoria, Queen 66
Vishnu 24, 37
Vivekananda 27

waka 105
Waley, Arthur 55
Wallis, John 176
Wang Chung-hui 85
Wang, C. T. 85
Wang Yang-ming 61
Ward, Frederick T. 71
Ward, William 40, 41
Washington, D. C. 120
Watts, Allan 24
Weber, Max 126, 173
Wellesley, Lord 43, 44
Western Chou period 53, 54
Western Clothing, Food, Houses 121
Wheaton, Henry 84
Whitney, General 141, 145, 146, 147
Widow Remarriage Act 40
Wilberforce, William 40
Williams, C. M. 135
Williams, S. Wells 112
World War I 82
World War II 97, 141, 142, 143
Wuchang Uprising 81
Wusung 76
Wylie, Alexander 84

Xavier, Francis 107

Yale University 85, 87
Yamato-damashi 97, 115, 150
Yangtse River 71, 156
Yaos 53, 55
Yedo 108, 111, 112, 114, 115, 120, 121
Yen, James 87, 88
Yen, W. S. 85
Yoga School 28
yogi 23, 31
Yokohama 112, 137, 138
Yokoi Shonan 118, 129
Young Men's Christian Association (YMCA) 85, 87, 90
Yu, Y. T. 91
Yuan dynasty 65
Yung-an 71
Yung Ming 85

Zen 14, 17, 106, 114, 125, 158